DOLOMITES

JOURNEY THROUGH AN ENCHANTED KINGDOM

CONTENTS

IN THE NORTH-EASTERN part of the Italian Alps is the geological jewel called the Dolomites, visited every year by millions who come to enjoy their rose-coloured peaks, unspoilt forests, verdant valleys, varied activities and fascinating culture.

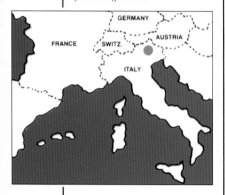

DUE TO THEIR central location in Europe, you can easily reach the Dolomites by car or plane, with the closest international airports being Venice, Treviso, Verona and Trieste. Once you arrive, an excellent road system links all the valleys and tourism centres.

THE VARIETY OF climates and rocks, the richness of vegetation and wildlife, the unique cultural enclaves, all set against the historical backdrop that nature and man have painted over the centuries - this is what makes the Dolomites unforgettable.
Our journey won't be limited to just the typical locations: we also have a lot of surprises in store!

● The Sorapis massif from Lake Misurina

THE ORIGINS OF A DREAM

The enchanting landscapes we see today conceal treasures of inestimable value. Whole chapters of a history dating back literally thousands of centuries - 270 million years of nature's mystical work.

MILLIONS OF YEARS AND THE EARTH'S DEEPEST ENERGY PUSHED UP THESE MASSIVE BLOCKS FROM THE OCEAN, TO BE HEWED BY THE ELEMENTS' SCULPTING HANDS.

THE FOSSILS

"A characteristic of dolomitic rock is that, unlike other parts of the Alps where fossilisation took place by organic compounds transforming into stone, in this region the animal and plant remains dissolved, leaving behind their imprints and moulds." The splendid Megalodonte, a mollusc that flourished here 220 million years ago, is just one example of the fossils found in the region. They vary from a few centimetres to almost a metre across - perhaps you will find one on your trip!

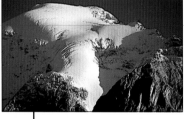

THE GLACIERS

The ice ages cast their frozen spell across the area, with mantles over 1,500 metres thick. And in the milder interglacial times, the rocks were chiselled by the elements, creating new valleys, lakes and remote, high- level eternal glaciers.

Plant life was always the first to return, taking a precarious foothold in between the barren rocks.

Let's start with the Triassic age, 250 million years ago, and the warm Tethys sea bed, rich with seaweed, molluscs, fish and coral. The earth's tectonic plate movements pushed together the areas of today's Africa and Europe, with volcanic eruptions, fractures and folding that uplifted the area. The sea gradually withdrew, exposing the sea bed with its crustacea and fish as lasting testimony to its presence. Thus the Dolomites emerged, their skyward ascent faster than the process of erosion which, in the millennia to come, would carve the landscape we see today: spires, massifs, sheer rock faces, and beside them - as if to complement their majesty - the valleys, with their softer outlines eroded by water as opposed to sharper frost-etched shapes of the peaks.

• right: the Sassolungo

THE NAME "DOLOMITES"

derives from the rock's first "official" scholar, the French geologist Déodat-Guy-Sylvain-Tancrè de Gratet de Dolomieu (1750-1801), who in 1789 was so fascinated by the carbonate rock of the area that he sent samples to Switzerland for classification. These were returned along with the announcement that their geological composition-hitherto unknown-warranted their naming after the "founder". In the 19th century, it was largely the English tourists who applied the original "Dolomia" name more widely to the extension of its geological area.

DOLOMITE

rock is made up of stratified calcium magnesium carbonate, with some areas of purer limestone. Depending on the area, some parts are more stratified and folded than others and contain thick layers of seaweed, coral and other organisms that lived in the ancient Tethys Sea.

When the last ice age receded only about 15,000 years ago, the area was at last able to sustain life. And as if by magic, plants, insects and animals gradually began to populate the land.

The water and soil on the valley floors allowed forests to take root, reaching right up to the snow line or the bare rock faces.

The broad pasture land in the valleys today is the outcome of man's work in recent centuries. At first, the scree and debris taken down from the peaks left the valley sides stony and barren and it was only with time that organic remains in the earth allowed vegetation to grow up the slopes.

The typical trees of the mountain landscape are the fir and larch in the valleys and the hardier pine higher up. To picture just how the post-glacial landscape might have looked, go up to a high plateau, where only some flowers live in these conditions, together with some types of moss.
Along with the vegetation came the animals which quickly became part of life in the valleys and mountains: chamois goats, long-horned mountain goats, roe deer, marmots and many other animals are still found in this region; an ideal habitat between the chill north and the milder climate of the Mediterranean.
Imagine taking only a few seconds to travel back in time thousands of years - like in a film sequence where the sun rises and sets in only a few seconds - to witness nature's reawakening.

Listen to the sounds filling the air: the rush of the streams and rivers, the chatter of birds, the rustle of branches in the wind and the gallop of a family of chamois goat (photo p.13); behold the inspiring vision of an eagle, its wing tips carving across the sapphire skies.

YOU CAN FIND

the varieties of plants and flowers of the Dolomites in many books, with excellent renditions of their beauty produced in pictures and paintings. Yet there is nothing better than to see nature's work in situ, on the meadows or upper slopes: multicoloured miracles, seemingly dainty, yet models of hardiness.

● Dawn on the brink of the horizon

● left: the Tofane at sunset

● snow sprinkling the Croda da Lago

TOWARDS THE END OF THE LAST ICE AGE, *the area must have been far from hospitable. The first men who ventured here were probably hunters and trappers from the plains in search of animals to eat and skin. At the end of the summer season, they would return to the plain and valleys to trade their catch for utensils and other items.*

Notes

The highest burial chamber in Europe: at Mondeval, 2,000 metres above sea level, a green plateau between Cortina and Colle S. Lucia. Here, under the overhang of a large rock, the remains were found of what is believed to be a tribal chief. Perhaps he was the best hunter of a people who came here 8,000 years ago during the Mesolythic period to hunt deer and large mountain goats. It's well worth a visit to the museum of Selva di Cadore, where you can see the remains themselves and the man's burial chattels.

ALONG THE MEADOWS

Stroll along the slopes in the twilight and you may spot an owl - motionless as it surveys its domain - or perhaps a sprightly squirrel. And if you see a roe deer that stops to return your glance, time will seem to stand still for those few moments.

The woods gradually overflowed with the flora and fauna which we can appreciate and enjoy today. On the footpaths above 1600 metres, you can see chamois goats grazing the scant grass between the rocks; you can hear the marmot's call; while driving, a deer may cross the road, its eyes showing fright before springing lightly away into the trees. But the most striking sight is that of an eagle majestically sweeping across the sky, surveying in slow circles every centimetre below, every bush and branch: impassive guardian and queen of the mountains. Many parts of the Dolomites have been designated Nature Parks (or *Parchi Naturali*) and have of course become the favourite habitats for many species of animals and birds. In some parts of the Parks, even the alpine brown bear still roams, now nearly extinct throughout western Europe. But there are many other animals that are easy to spot on walks in the woods or higher up among the rocky tundra. Make sure you take your binoculars! The majestic eagle is not alone in the skies. Many varieties of birds fill the air and expert eyes can distinguish the alpine chough, which flies in small flocks above the summits; the woodland grouse or capercaillie, which feels safer in the woods and undergrowth;

and the white ptarmigan, which vaunts a brown plumage in the summer. Perhaps the commonest birds are the crows: when perched on the grass at the forest edge, they appear almost as jet-black flowers cropping up in clusters on the green. When walking through the woods you may be lucky enough to see, as well as hear, the woodpecker, preoccupied with his work, the Alpine tree-creeper, the jay, the skylark and many species of finch.
Ever since the valleys became inhabited, their wildlife has been an important element for the population's livelihood. Although sheep and dairy farming are no longer the main source of income for most people, sheep and cattle still best characterise these mountain communities."

● A pair of chamois

● A curious buck deer

IN THE SPRING

the mountains literally throng with life. Everything has its own rhythm, which slows down in winter to come alive again in the spring.

● A rare sight of a lynx

● A roe deer

When littered with languidly grazing livestock, the upper pastures evoke a peace that seems to open a window in time back to the last century, or perhaps even much earlier, when the entire Dolomite region was one enormous pasture.

The old community, whose livelihood was based on sheep farming alone, has been superseded. But it has left the mountain dwellers with a vital legacy for the future: that animals and wildlife in general are very precious heritage and should be actively protected along with their habitat. It is this profound respect for nature that has led to the opening of so many *Parchi Naturali* in the Dolomites: the Sesto Natural Park in Val Pusteria; the Fanes-Sennes-Prags-Braies Natural Park straddling the Val d'Ampezzo, Val Badia and Val Pusteria; the Adamello-Brenta Natural Park in the far southwest; the Puèz-Odle Natural Park between Val Gardena and Val di Funes; the Paneveggio-Pale di San Martino Natural Park in Val Cordevole; the Sciliar-Alpe di Siusi Natural Park near Bolzano; and the Ampezzo Park at Cortina

- are all testimonies to the people's determination to protect the Dolomites from that facet of progress which can damage nature's work. The landscapes and panoramas, the flowers, plants, animals and birds are all privileged, in today's frenetic climate, to be left alone in their natural habitat - so many parts of the Dolomites truly are, then, an enchanted garden.

● Chamois tracks

● Night predator

UNTIL THE END OF THE LAST CENTURY, *bears commonly inhabited the woods of the Dolomites, but deforestation and hunting took their toll and their numbers declined. While for many years they were thought to be extinct almost throughout the region, hope has recently been rekindled with the discovery of bear tracks in the area of Sappada. Researchers believe the bears may have migrated gradually from across the Slovenian border where the breed still flourishes.*

THE CHAMOIS GOATS *can be more easily seen in winter, against the snow covered pastures when they move down towards the valleys to seek easier grazing pastures. Chamois are not as timid as the long-horned wild mountain goats (photo p. 90), or "stambecchi", perhaps because they always move in groups.*

● Chamois on the move

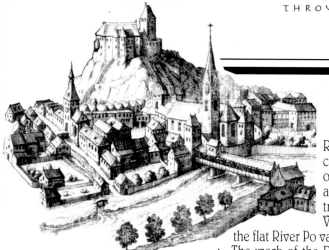

The Romans called the inhabitants of the Alps the Rhaetians of whom debate continues as to their ethnic origin, and who lived in the area between the Germanic tribes to the north and the Venetians and Etruscans in the flat River Po valley to the south.

The work of the Roman proconsul Quintus Marcius - King of the Stoeni - marked the beginning of Rome's power in the region, at first only west of the river Adige valley, to gradually extend eastward.

It was not an untroubled conquest: the raids of the Cimbrians from the north, up the Isarco and Adige valleys in 102 BC, forced the Roman troops installed at Tridentum - today's Trento - to retreat. The all-powerful Romans had however made their breach, thus opening the way for Drusus and Tiberius - Caesar Augustus's step-sons - to lead the campaign which brought all the main valleys of the Dolomites under Rome.

Contact between the various valleys was much facilitated by two important roads: the Claudia Augusta Padana, along the Adige valley, and the Claudia Augusta Altinate, from Feltre to the Val Pusteria.

This period gave birth to the fascinating Ladin language - a highly evocative blend of Latin and the original Rhaetian language - which is still spoken in its local variations in the Dolomites today.

HISTORICALLY,

the Dolomites have largely served as a buffer zone between the Germanic and Mediterranean peoples. When travelling in the Dolomites, you can see many castles, fortresses and other strategic emplacements the function of which - located as they are at the valley mouths, perched on lofty ledges or perhaps spread along steep slopes - was to control the passage to the area.

The effect these military installations had on human geography was to encourage hamlets and towns to grow up close by and under their protection.

● A Gothic altar

● Prösels Castle

Before this century, travel was a wholly different experience. A journey of only 20 km either meant hours on the back of a horse, mule or donkey, or being jolted along in a carriage. The unmade roads and the other unknown surprises possibly lying in wait, travel was not to be undertaken lightly. But, for the Roman Empire at its height, these valleys represented a vital link to colonising the north, a connection it consolidated in no uncertain terms.

The first century AD was marked by the population of Trentino being recognised as Roman citizens. An imperial ambassador was appointed as governor of Rhaetia and Italy's imperial boundaries were thus extended as far as the Danube. But Rome's power soon became threatened by the barbarian populations pushing southwards from various parts.

Attila's Huns, Theodoric's Ostrogoths, the Longobards, the Franks and Bavarians, all attacked the area in the first millennium after Christ - and indeed succeeded in occupying various zones in different phases. It was perhaps this very subjection to different regimes over time that engendered a spirit of independence in the local population. Thus came about the institution of the Liberi Comuni (Free Municipalities) or the Magnifiche Comunità (Magnificent Communities), which have maintained their authority - largely unchanged - in such towns as Trento, Feltre, Belluno and Bolzano, or indeed whole valleys, like Cadore, Fiemme, Agordino and Ampezzo.

As we will see later in this book, the Church was important in shaping the area's history. From the early years of 1000 onwards, it played a part that was just as political as it was spiritual, and, like all political roles, it was supported at different times by both the central governments and the nobility-backed independent feudal movements. The result was that the Dolomites continued to be the theatre of rivalry between the Guelphs and the Ghibellines, between bishops, Tyrolese counts, small feudatories, imperial governors and local independent bodies. By the end of the 13th century, this rich melting pot had boiled down to the bishops and counts being under the domination of the House of Hapsburg and the Duke of Austria.

THE CHURCH

represented a strong political and spiritual power in the history of the Dolomites: after the rule of Charlemagne and the Treaty of Verdun - which in 843 divided the Dolomites between the Italian and Germanic reigns - the bishoprics were created. As is borne out by the important and still standing Episcopal buildings, the bishops of Trento and Bressanone had most of the northern and western Dolomites under their jurisdiction, while the southern and eastern parts were consigned to the Churches of Feltre and Aquileia. The ecclesiastical principalities were generally the "long arm" of the central government used as a bulwark against the independent feudal forces.

Notes

**You may well wonder why St. Christopher is so often portrayed on the façades of the mountain churches.
As the protector of travellers, his image was certainly a reassuring icon for pilgrims and wayfarers for whom these parts were so little known and potentially dangerous, not only for their harsh winter climate but also for the disconcerting tales and fables so often associated with them.**

● Looking towards the Siusi plateau

At the beginning of the 15th century the process began that was to divide the areas of Germanic influence from those under Venetian domination. The Hapsburgs retained control over the central-northern region, which adopted not only their political organisation but also their language, while the south-eastern zone became part of Venice's Serenissima Republic. Although the Ampezzo valley had to cede to the Tyrol, the area of Cadore remained under Venetian dominion, as did Trento, through the efforts of bishop Bernardo Clesio, who was decidedly in favour of the "Italian" power. Bishop Clesio fostered the Renaissance artistic currents typical of the courts of the Italian princes and indeed it was under his mandate that the church of S. Maria Maggiore was built, followed by the Magno Palazzo, the Geremia, Tabarelli and other typically Renaissance period buildings. The Serenissima Republic also played a part in promoting the expansion of the new architectural criteria, in particular at Belluno and Feltre, but also at Agordo. With defence remaining the keystone to social organisation, new castles and fortresses were constructed throughout the Dolomite region.

● The Novacella monastery

OVER THE CENTURIES,

all kinds of fortifications have been built in the Dolomites, a necessity brought about by the countless threats from all sides due to the area's strategic position as 'buffer' between very different civilisations. What better solution then, than to exploit the mountains' physical attributes and erect castles on the rocky outcrops at the valley mouths, to control access to the town right from the outposts. Today the castles and fortresses in the Dolomites conserve the allure of those times. If you enter one and look out from an upper window, you can let yourself be taken back centuries and picture the smith's carriage in the courtyard below, bumping along the cobbled street bound for the next village, the local master's house, or perhaps the ecclesiastical authority that defends "his" valley from incursions.

● The old main street of Brunico

● right: Monguelfo Castle

LOCAL COSTUMES

have changed little over the centuries and are still worn today at weddings and other traditional occasions. They are a source of great pride for the people of these valleys, who genuinely love to keep in touch with their past.

TRADITIONAL FESTIVALS

vary from one village to another, especially in some of the valleys where, as a reaction to the assaults of the Twentieth Century, cultural identities have become even more deeply rooted in the local customs. And yet they all share similarly blended origins: between the sacred and the secular, the ancient propitiatory rites of nature and the religious festivals of patron saints. At the S. Vigilio festival in Trento, for example, the famous Palio dell'Oca ("goose's prize") is held.

W hen Napoleon arrived in the Dolomites in the 18th century, the characteristics of the inhabitants had already been defined, with a very clear distinction between the areas under Tyrolese domination, the Italian irredentists and those under individual local protection. These were the years when the territory began to be systematically exploited, when Dèodat de Dolomieu discovered the unique rock that was to be named after him, and when the echo of the area's beauty rippled abroad, to as far afield as England. Agriculture and live-stock were the traditional sources of income for the Dolomite valleys, and the local laws regulating them date back to equally early times. One example was the regola del Maso Chiuso (rule of the 'closed valley farm') of Austro-Germanic origin, which established that the entire farm property, together with the right to use its surrounding land, be passed down to a single heir, thus ensuring that the means for supporting a whole family was preserved.

D uring the chill winter months when work in the fields was limited, the people made best use of their time by making things with their hands. Thus began a handicraft tradition that included iron work and the production of nails but which also flourished into specialist wood carving and engraving, woodworking in general, embroidery and weaving of cloths for local costumes. Perhaps the fact that the area has suffered so much foreign rule is what has led the local traditions - although sometimes very different - to be so strenuously upheld. On the feast days of patron saints and other village festivals, everyone is very conscientious about wearing their traditional costumes and repeating the dances and motions that have been handed down for centuries by their forebears, to ensure their precious treasure does not get swept away by the haste of modern life.

● A veil of low-level cloud over the hamlet of Ornella

● right: Colz Castle in Val Badia

At the turn of the century, along with the many ethnic and political conflicts, two major events were to mark the Dolomites forever: the two World Wars, which were heroically fought amongst these very rocks and slopes; and the advent of tourism as one of the primary sources of income for much of the region. The sudden influx of tourists naturally had much to do with the improvement of the railways and roads. From as early as the mid 19th century, the greatest mountaineering enthusiasts from Europe tested their wits and skills in opening new paths and approaches to the summits.

In Cortina, Paul Grohmann, accompanied by local guides, scaled the previously unconquered summits of Tofana di Rozes, Tofana di Fuori, and Tofana di Mezzo, as well as

Sorapis and Cristallo. At the turn of the century, the Innerkofler guides of Sesto led many expeditions to the Tre Cime and the Tre Scarperi. All regions of the Dolomites began to be frequented by other kinds of tourism: from the well-to-do but sporting families (mainly from Britain and Austria) to those of a more aristocratic and elite disposition. A hundred years of catering to tourism has given the Dolomite region the kind of experience which today enables them to vaunt the very best facilities and hospitality.

● The centre of Ortisei

● The Lagazuoi cable car

A LOT HAS CHANGED

since the 1850s when the first Alpine pioneers began to set their sights on the enigmatic peaks of the Dolomites. The advances in walking and climbing equipment have brought with them an added safety and comfort to approaching the mountains on foot.
By far the easiest way to reach the top is of course by cable car: while the thrill of conquest is less than from an unaided hike to the summit, the speed of the ascent as it changes your perspective on the surrounding panorama is certain to create an unforgettable experience.

● Hiking towards the Scotoni peak

Bank Banca

In summer and winter alike, the Dolomite valleys offer a seemingly inexhaustible supply of beauty, amenities and events. The over 100 high-level mountain refuges, or *rifugi*, scattered in invariably unique panoramic locations, provide some of the greatest pleasures to mountain lovers.

With their rustic charm and unparalleled hospitality, the refuges beckon all visitors, whether arriving on foot, by climbing, or simply by chair - lift or car - to seek rejuvenation of the body and soul. An elixir made from pure alpine air and that love for the mountains which brings together everyone, what-ever their language, race or creed.

With hotels and restaurants catering to all tastes and budgets, the people of the towns and villages pride themselves in their hospitality. And of course if you're looking for an even more authentic local atmosphere, you can find excellent accommodation in the smallest, family-run *pensioni*.

No matter the season, a wealth of activities awaits you: from the hiking o the summer to the Alpine- and cross-country skiing in winter; from bird-watching to climbing; from a mountain-bike ride to powder skiing; from flower watching (no picking, please!) to photography. A bounty of beauty and excitement to be enjoyed and shared!

● Panoramic deck at Sasso Pordoi

● Town centre of San Martino di Castrozza

● Malga Ra Stua, between Cortina and Dobbiaco

● Souvenirs

● Sunday in the square

OVER 100 REFUGES AND HUTS

are dotted around the Dolomites which, although serving mainly to refresh the mountaineer after a walk or a climb, are usually in locations with breathtaking views. Which is why we highly recommend spending a night in a rifugio, to take in the sunset and sunrise against an unforgettable Alpine backdrop.

While the type of accommodation often means sleeping in four or more to a room, the sporting atmosphere is second to none enough to soften up even the most diffident of tourists!

In front of the hearth over supper, while enjoying a hot bowl of barley soup, you can get to know many people from all walks of life - but all enlivened by the invigorating mountain air.

ANCIENT ROADS

Our journey begins in the Val Pusteria or "Green Valley", one of the ancient east-west routes used since time immemorial. These woods, meadows and rock faces have seen countless travellers pass by over the years.

SINCE ROMAN TIMES, THE VALLEY WAS USED BY PEOPLE FROM AGUNTUM - EAST OF LIENZ - TRAVELLING ALONG THE CLAUDIA AUGUSTA ALTINATE ROAD.

Just to the south of the Austrian border, running from Bressanone (Brixen) in the west to Lienz in the east, is the Val Pusteria (German name "Pustertal"). The valley is rich in local history, legend, wartime memories and Alpine adventures, and today is imbued with the serenity of its lush green pastures. This area of the Dolomites literally has something for everyone: for those with a passion for the past, the oldest monastery of the Dolomites stands at San Candido, now the Museum of the Collegiate; and if you enjoy delving into the charm of fables, it is said that in these mountains were under the reign of the legendary King Laurino. As to more concrete history, this area was the scene of bitter front battles during the First World War, and many of the summits are still riddled with tunnels and military installations dug out or dynamited by Italian and Austrian soldiers. This is also the valley of the Innerkoflers, the great mountaineers who guided the first important ascents of the century. And yet the Pusteria valley is also home to gentle slopes, lush meadows and charming villages. Here we are in the heart of the South Tyrol and the strong Austrian traits are for all to see: from the language - more German than Italian - to the style of the homes and local traditions.

FROM SESTO TO BOLZANO
Sesto
Moso
S.Candido
Dobbiaco
Anterselva
Val di Casies
Val di Braies
Monguelfo
Villabassa
Valdaora
Brunico
Val di Tures
Valle Aurina
S.Lorenzo
Maranza
Fundres
Bresanone
Chiusa
Bolzano

● The Cima Dodici (literally the Twelve o'Clock Peak)   ● photo right: Chiusa and the monastery at Sabiona

THE TRE SCARPERI
(photo below) are famous features of the Pusteria valley, along with its lush meadows and characteristic masi or valley farms.

Although part of Italy since 1919, the Val Pusteria is a boundary area, with the Austrian border cutting across its eastern part. At this end is Dobbiaco and the small town of San Candido, from where the Val di Sesto extends south eastwards, coasting the Austrian boundary.

For generations the name Innerkofler has been synonymous with Alpine guides. Associated with the valley's most important mountaineering feats, both sporting and wartime, these exceptional men were enlisted to play their part on the hapless stage of combat in desperate winter conditions. Apart from the tragic memories they hold, these peaks also hold faint echoes of the first intrepid adventurers to scale them. The names of the surrounding peaks though - Cima Nove, Cima Dieci, Cima Undici (Peak Nine, Peak Ten, etc.) - are not to celebrate a sequence of climbing accomplishments;

rather, they signify the notches of a gigantic natural sundial.

The Sesto valley leads south west from San Candido, its villages of Sesto and Moso, with their white houses and ornaments in the windows, re-evoking the refined and elegant contours of the mountains. Here too the community has a strongly Austrian feel to it.

We are only barely inside Italy at just a few kilometres from the

Austrian border. As recently as 1919 this area was well within Austria, a history reflected of course in the predomination of Tyrolese traditions in culture and costume.

Place names and road signs are always bilingual and the Italian spoken has a distinct Austrian lilt. The local history and heritage are strongly tinged with collective dignity and everyone plays a part in upholding this precious tradition.

• Sesto di Pusteria looking south-west to the Punta Tre Scarperi

• Typical Tyrolese decorations

The beauty of the upper Val Pusteria lies as much in its enchanting yet distant peaks as in its slopes, which descend so gracefully to the valley floor. The peace of the green curves, interspersed with the large isolated farm houses, or masi, is complemented by the view of the snow-capped peaks overlooking the town of San Candido (Innichen). Both have their own story to tell, the crests with their natural evolution, the slopes more manmade. As far back as during the first millennium, the mountain slopes were deforested

SAN CANDIDO,
on the flat valley floor of the Val Pusteria, is an ancient settlement that was one of the most important centres of Alto Adige. In 769, the Bavarian duke Tassilone III founded a Benedictine abbey there, where today stands the Duomo della Collegiata, considered the "Romanesque jewel of the Tyrol".

to allow livestock grazing and, with it, the food and dairy products for the valley's inhabitants. And the masi, built at feudatory expense, were used to provide shelter and storage space for the animals and folk.

In keeping with the old ways, the masi are still used and inhabited, and stand as living heritage of an ancient chronicle.

The town of San Candido itself is a very pretty village just seven kilometres from the Austrian border and boasts much variety, between the history of its medieval churches and sites and an array of delightful shops facing onto the piazza. Today there are many guest houses and hotels - some with Tyrolese-style beer gardens with music - which, like the inns of old times, offer typical mountain hospitality and fare.

San Candido was once the centre of a region conferred to Abbot Otto di Scharnitz, on condition that he establish a Benedictine monastery to convert the Slavs who had settled there after the periods of conflict. While nothing remains of this earlier church, the *Duomo della Collegiata* stands in its place.

• San Candido and the Rocca dei Baranci

• The Holy Sepulchre chamber in the Altötting chapel

Notes

We highly recommend a visit to the chapel of Altötting close to the centre of San Candido (near the railway line). Although modest compared to the town's superb Romanesque church, it has a fascinating history: Georg Paprion built it as a scaled-down model of the Holy Sepulchre in Jerusalem, which he had seen in 1653 while on a pilgrimage to the Holy Land. The first chamber contains wooden statues modelled on the church of Altötting, while the inner room - with its granite arches and columns - contains the Sepulchre itself, with a prone wooden sculpture of Christ. In the summer season, the chapel is usually open every day from 10 am to midday and from 4 to 6 pm.

I n the parish church of Dobbiaco, among other south Tyrolese works of art, you can find the medieval tombstone depicting a judge and his wife in chains and in prayer. What strikes one most is the picture's content rather than its artistic value. The judge was enchained upon his own orders to expiate a grave sin he had committed: in 1500, during a feast in Herbstenburg Castle (at the centre of the old village), a guard announced to Judge Peitlestein that he had detained a vagabond. Somewhat the worse for wear from quaffing generous quantities of liquor, the judge ordered the man to be locked up in the Red Tower, saying that the following day he would attend to the matter.

But no one remembered the poor man for a whole week, whereupon he was found dead from thirst and starvation.

DOBBIACO

(photo below) lies on what was once a broad river bed.
Here it seems to nestle in a bed of yellow flowers, while the spring breeze ripples its surface like the waters of a magic sea.

O vercome by remorse, the judge went on a pilgrimage to Rome and carried with him, together with his wife, a chain around his neck.

The geographical position of Dobbiaco has been both the fortune and misfortune of the town: situated at a natural intersection between the Val Pusteria and Val di Landro connecting Cortina to the south, in ancient times Dobbiaco was where travellers stopped on their journeys to and from Venice. It later grew from just a stopover village to a resort in its own right for the Austrian and German nobility, who loved its setting: close to the lakes of Dobbiaco and Landro - from which it takes the name "duplex lacus" - the splendid surrounding peaks, and its green mountain pastures. Unfortunately, during the first World War, the houses of Dobbiaco - which were overlooked by the artillery on Mount Cristallo up the Landro valley - were destroyed by grenades, and its inhabitants had to fight many of the hardest and most decisive battles of the zone on nearby Monte Piana and the spectacular Tre Cime di Lavaredo.

● Dobbiaco, looking towards Val San Silvestro

● right: the Croda Rossa

LA CRODA ROSSA

takes its name ('Red Crag') from its rock, which in a certain light comes alive with a crimson hue. Visually imposing despite its distance from the village itself, the Croda Rossa appears to protect Dobbiaco with its almost grave air, rather like a castle with natural ramparts that belongs to a mysterious mountain god. Here, traditions, habits and customs have very ancient roots.

AT THE CROSSROADS OF TWO VALLEYS,

Dobbiaco has always been the place to stop for travellers from the Orient or between the Tyrol and Venice. Slavs and Bvarians fought over it in more ancient times, as did the Austrians and Italians in the early part of this century.

LAKE BRAIES,

lying like an emerald at the foot of the Croda del Becco, is completely surrounded by thick forest which descends to caress the water, and be magically mirrored in it.
We have now entered the fabulous Fanes-Sennes-Braies Nature Park, where modern life takes time out to reflect.

Notes

Although Lake Braies itself is renowned mostly for its ethereal beauty, its fascinating hotel dates back to the turn of the century. Later, in the sixties and seventies, it was brought into the international limelight when Yogi Mahraishi of Katmandu - the Beatles' personal guru - held his meditation courses there, with guests arriving from all over the world.

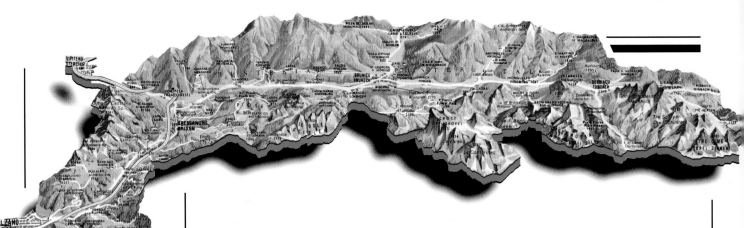

In the heart of the Val Pusteria, where the valleys of Aurina, Tures and Ora meet, is the splendid town of Brunico (Bruneck). It's an ancient town, built at the foot of a rocky spur on which its castle rises. Two concentric bands of coloured houses are elegantly placed against each other and decorated with "erkers", typical southern Tyrolese decorations.

The central shopping street divides these two bands of houses running along the ancient double wall that once served as a bulwark for the castle.
Only four arched wall gates afford access to this treasure trove: the Orsoline, Floriani, Rienza and Ragan di Sopra with their coloured frescoes hinting at the grace of the town within.

● Masi, the traditional farm houses, above Brunico

MANY CASTLES

were built in the area around Brunico due to the town's strategic position at the crossroads of four valleys: Castel San Michele, Castel Badia, Villa Ottone, Castel Tures (opposite photo) are just some examples. Today Brunico also administers the districts of S. Giorgio, Villa S. Caterina and San Lorenzo and Stegona. For a few days every year, the town stages its famous market fair, an attraction not to be missed if you're anywhere in the vicinity at the time!

● above: Brunico's ancient Via Centrale

● right: Campo Tures castle

EVEN IN THE PLACES
where you expect nature to provide the central attraction, like in the valleys near Brunico, it's not unusual to stumble upon beautiful works of local art.

IT WAS THE COPPER
miners of the Aurina valley who wanted to have the Church of the Holy Spirit built beyond Predoi and Casera, and who made the necessary donations for it to be constructed. They had lived happy times, mining excellent quality copper ore that was taken from Predoi to Cadipietra to be refined by the Aurina mining company. But at the end of the 18th century, American copper produced at much lower costs swamped the market, thus ending the era of copper mining in the valley.

The Brunico district has a wealth of legends and traditions. One tale tells of a farmer from Sares who found a small black Madonna in a ploughed field. He took it home and put it near the hearth but the following day it had gone. After searching high and low, he found it on a nearby knoll, where he built a shrine that still stands to this day.

In October a large fair is held at Stegona, now a district of Brunico. The first days are mostly for the locals to discuss their business for the coming winter, while in the last days formality is thrown to the wind and the place becomes a stage for a full-scale festival: fun, entertainment, dancing, wurstels, mulled wine and local beer, all whirling into a colourful festival for all.

On leaving the bustle of Brunico you need only drive up one of the side valleys to be plunged again into nature's unspoilt beauty: north from the town, up the Val di Tures, is the striking contrast of the steep valley sides with the broadness of the valley floor, where the Aurino mountain stream wends its way southwards to join the main valley.

● *Farm house at Riva di Tures*

These gentle meadows and flowing waters belie what is only just upstream, where steep slopes and rushing torrents provide the scene as you pass Campo Tures. Situated where the valley divides into the Val di Riva and Valle Aurina, Tures Castle (built in about 1200) was renovated in 1907 and is now open to the public.

Both the valleys widen as they extend up amongst steep rocks, remote lakes and mountain pastures, where the air resounds with the rush of the torrents. The villages and hamlets are tidy, well ordered and effortlessly picturesque. There are crafts workshops producing a range of engraved wood items. Tourism is gradually becoming more popular because these valleys offer the possibility of savouring something of the ancient farming spirit.

This zone belongs to the massif of central gneiss, the first blocks of dolomitic rock formed when it emerged from the ancient Tethys sea. Something of those distant times seems to have rubbed off onto people, who are somewhat disinclined to adopt some of life's modern comforts. To forge a way into the valley of Aurina, the rock had to be mined and blasted, so the road hugs the sides of the mountain up along the banks of the sinuous stream.

• View towards the church of S. Spirito

• The Aurina valley

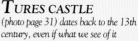

TURES CASTLE

(photo page 31) dates back to the 13th century, even if what we see of it today is the result of meticulous restoration and extension work carried out in 1907. With its 64 rooms, 24 of which completely decked out in wood, the Castel di Tures has everything one would expect of an ancient castle: it is furnished with valuable antique furniture and adorned with glass artwork, sculptures, paintings and other precious ornaments.

The arms gallery contains a fine collection of harquebuses, perhaps the very ones used in the war against the Turks and depicted on the splendid majolica stove in the castle library. The Romanesque chapel is also well worth the visit, with frescoes by Michael Pacher from Brunico.

AT THE BOTTOM OF THE AURINA VALLEY

rises the Vetta d'Italia.
You may wonder why it is called the "Peak of Italy" since the mountain stands at 2912 metres compared to the 3498 m of the nearby Picco dei Tre Signori.
The reason is simply that it is at the northernmost point of Italy.
Only the most determined hikers venture up along the ancient footpaths of the upper pastures.

KING LAURINO

forgot to curse the roses of his garden at sunset, which is why the Catinaccio massif takes on such strongly pink hues at sunset.

S. CIPRIANO

(photo right) is just one of the many tiny chapels nestling in the valleys to the east of the Isarco valley. Some are even private, like the one standing at the foot of the Odle in Val di Funes (photo below).

When you leave the western end of Val Pusteria to enter the broad Isarco valley, it's like leaving a cosy room to step out into a splendid spring day, where you can fill your lungs with the fresh air of the brand new season.

Heading south, the scenery rolls by and you can enjoy the mountains, like the Plose, as they appear farther in the distance: a few kilometres south of Bressanone is the entrance to the Val di Funes, with its villages, meadows, woods, and many chapels - some of which private. Farther south down the Isarco valley are the approaches to three more valleys: the Val Gardena, the Val di Tires and the Val d'Ega. The latter two lead to the area of the Catinaccio, or Rosengarten, and what better place to stop and admire the kingdom of the mythical King Laurino than beside Lake Carezza (photo right).

S till and translucent, its waters buffed lightly by the breeze, Lago di Carezza lies amidst thick firs, watched over by the jagged walls of the Latemar range. How to get there? About mid-way between Bolzano and Canazei, just to the west of the Passo di Costalunga col which connects the Val d'Ega with the Val di Fassa.

• The Catinaccio massif

• The San Cipriano chapel

• The Odle crests from the Val di Funes

right: the emerald Lago di Carezza

Brixen.

While enjoying the area's natural wonders, take time to visit one of the Dolomites' oldest town centres: Bressanone (or Brixen). Its porticoed streets are a delight to stroll through, whether you're a local history buff or just interested in browsing the shops and cafes. Many of the stores in the old centre were once workshops of craftsmen who created some of the most refined hand-made furniture and other handicraft items of the region. In the cathedral of S. Vergine, with its cloister and ancient cemetery, you will find such artistic icons as the symbolic frescoes, some of which by Paul Troger.

Recent restoration work has actually brought to light three

NOVACELLA

The monumental complex of buildings of the Novacella monastery - with the chapel of San Michele (photo below) standing at its entrance - was commissioned in 1142 by the Bishop of Bressanone, Artmano, and Reginberto of Sabione, for the Agostinian canons.

Under threat of invasion from the Turks, the chapel was fortified with an enclosing wall towards the end of the 15th century.

In 1735 the abbey church of the Madonna, which was originally Romanesque, was restructured in Baroque style. Inside you can see the exceptional stuccoes influenced by the rococo style.

● Novacella Abbey

● The Three Kings' Homage. Michael Parth 1520

layers of fresco works, the earliest dating as far back as to the 13th century.

Continuing our trip through Bressanone's past, we are drawn immediately to the Hofburg bishopric, where the architecture and diocesan museum testify to the importance the clergy played in the town's history. There is also a museum of nativity scenes, with a host of small statues carved skilfully by local craftsmen over the centuries.

Bressanone once represented the union between the basins of the rivers Adige and Danube along the ancient trading routes. During the early years of the century, it began to take advantage of its tourist appeal and became the cultural centre that so aptly characterises it today.

A stroll from the old town centre outwards to the first fields is just the job for relaxing while toning up: from the central medieval ring of tall buildings with their multicoloured façades, you can leave the walled centre through the gates, to pass among some later Baroque and Renaissance architecture and eventually reach the countryside beyond.

No matter whether your perspective begins from the outside or inside, the scene is embellished by an ever present backdrop of majestic mount Plose (2486 m), Bressanone's grand mountain.

• 14th century frescoes

THE PORTICOES IN THE EVENING

Since earliest times, the town was divided into an "Episcopal" and "lay" district, the latter being the heart of the commercial centre where the porticoes served as shelter for the activities of the tradesmen and artisans. The town was born under the auspices of the Bishops, who had chosen the location for its political and strategic virtues, which explains why the religious monuments are invariably splendid works of art.

Notes

Like all regions of Italy, cooking in the Dolomites offers a range of its own specialities and you can spoil yourself by trying a different dish every day. Although not elaborate, the food is always very tasty with the traditional fare dating back mainly to the eighteenth century when the staple ingredients were mixed, and available herbs and spices were used to blend the flavours.
Make sure you leave some room for the desserts and pastries: we recommend the strudel or the fritelle con panna e marmellata di mirtilli (doughnuts with fresh cream and blueberry jam).

• Evening in Bressanone's main street

*E*VEN BACK IN *the last century, the pyramids of Renon must have captured the imagination of artists, whose used their brushes to "photograph" the spectacular sight on canvas (print below). The towers are formed when large, solid rocks protect the underlying glacial moraine. The effect of wind, frost and rain erodes the surrounding earth, leaving the pyramids standing above. When the protecting rock eventually topples, the softer material rapidly erodes away. What kind of sculptures will be reserved for our grandchildren to discover?*

I t's as if you had entered into a grove of petrified trees or a forest of clay giants when you walk along the footpath around the piramidi di Renon (the "Pyramids of Renon") on the plateau above Bolzano. Instead it's nothing other than one of nature's whims: in post-glacial times, rocks, pebbles, shale and morainic material were pressed together amongst layers of clay. Over the years, the action of rain and snow carried away the softer material except for the areas protected by stones, thus leaving the stone perched on the pedestal of the material it protects. When the stones topple, nature's elements soon do their work to crumble the column down to mud and stones. The Renon plateau is not just a scene of nature's most curious work: it's also a favourite resort for the people from Bolzano, who come up in summer by a local train to Collalbo and the other villages for some respite from the balmy heat of the valley floor.

• One of the "pyramids" close up

Notes

These are certainly not the pyramids of El Giza! But a visit to the piramidi di Renon is a must if you are in the area.
It's best to go on a dry day because the area can be rather slippery when it rains.
Take the road from Bolzano west and drive up to the Renon plateau. A few kilometres up, you will find the glacial moraine exposed among the lush greenery (see explanation in main text).
It's worth taking a little more time to discover the most beautiful ones to the nort: hidden amongst the trees, they stand aloof like stone sculptures.

• Nineteenth century print

• right: the pyramids of Longomoso on the Renon uplands

Bozen

IN THE HEART

of Bolzano is the district of the pretty porticoed streets: a medieval shopping arcade that also hosts the homes of the shopkeepers themselves. In the traditional style of the Tyrol, the facàdes of the shops have been painted in different colours, recalling an era in Bolzano's history when, with its spectacular streets and elegant walks, it was known as the favourite 'jewel' of the archduchess Claudia de Medici, wife of Leopold, the Hapsburg sovereign of the Tyrol.

• Bolzano centre with the silhouette of Neptune's statue

Bolzano (Bozen) is the largest centre of the north-western Dolomites.
Of strongly Germanic culture, the town's historic importance stems largely from its strategic position. The main street is called Via dei Portici where the shop owners used to be called the 'kings of the porticoes'. Bolzano is a very lively town with something for everyone: shopping, sightseeing, and history. An interesting visit is to see the frescoes in the castles of Runkelstein and Roncolo, which, rather than depicting religious scenes, portray the most everyday events of the times. Archduchess Claudia - widow of Leopold of Hapsburg and queen of the Tyrol - loved the town and defined it appropriately as the region's "most precious jewel."

Bolzano has always been an important trading centre and cross-roads for the north and south and today the Via dei Portici still reflects this cultural confluence, with mainly German shops to the north and Italian ones to the south. Another unique result of this

• Ancient frescoes

Notes

**The shops in the bustling via Portici have preserved the ancient structure with their royal-, single- and double vaults.
As you stroll between the pillars it's as if you had stepped back in time.
Standing beneath the porticoes, with their columns standing solid and squat, if you tune your imagination, you will hear the cries of merchants, the clatter of the carriages and hooves on the cobbled streets, with the horses dressed in their tournament harnesses.**

• Façades of Bolzano's Baroque buildings

ALONG THE ANCIENT ROADS

long trading history is the host of different plants, shrubs and trees in the parks and villa gardens. Brought up from the south over the centuries by the well-to-do residents of the town, this flora can be enjoyed on a stroll in the Guancina gardens, which evoke a decidedly Mediterranean oasis set amongst the area's indigenous flora. Bolzano also enjoys a mild climate which has favoured the

scene described by Goethe in one of his travel diaries.

Although the vineyards are much smaller today than in the last century due to the town's encroachment for housing use, the local wine is still rounded, fragrant, and ideal as an aperitivo in one of the traditional osterie in the old town.

The historic centre of Gries with its flower-festooned villas was also incorporated into modern Bolzano.

DRINKING WINE

from one's own vineyard was considered one of the eight worldly pleasures of the inhabitants of Bolzano. The others? Having their own bench at the parish church, a house and a shop in via Portici, a villa on the Renon plateau, a box at

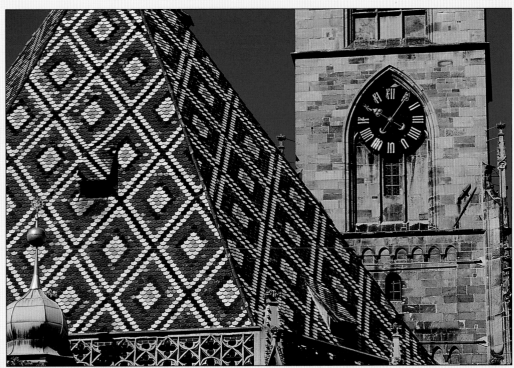

the theatre, a wife from a well-to-do neighbouring family, enough linen to last for six months, and a family tomb. This was how the chronicler Karl Theodor Hoeniger depicted the typical inhabitants of Bolzano in the last century. Today there are few who can afford this kind of lifestyle, but the list gives a picture of the elegant and fun loving nature of the people. It's the same spirit that you will come across in the town's streets, shops and osterie (inns) and in the workshops and cultural events staged in the piazza.

construction of thermal baths and health centres. The social life of the locals is very much centred on its square, which has been named after the medieval poet Walther von der Vogelweide. Piazza Walther is the *salotto* or 'lounge' of Bolzano where you can take in the atmosphere of the ancient square and perhaps enjoy one of the many events held there in throughout the year.

The Piazza della Mostra (literally "Exhibition Square") is enriched by the comely gothic façàde of Palazzo Campofranco. And in the Piazza del Municipio ("Town Hall Square") come together the streets with the best shops of the town.

To get to the 'real' daily life of the town, you must go to Piazza delle Erbe, with its fruit, vegetable and flower stalls, a memorable

Some local landmarks are the Victory Arch (Arco della Vittoria), a fascist monument that was hotly contested in 1928, the Talvera, one of Bolzano's two rivers, and the Monastery of the Benedictine monks of Muri-Gries.

The baroque church at Gries contains some works by Martin Knoller, which seem to challenge this evolution.

Perhaps Bolzano's most striking symbol is its cathedral, which flaunts a sandstone clock tower and a roof that seems embroidered (centre photo). Last but not least is the recently renovated and extended parish church, which is said to have been built on the spot where a carter discovered a picture of the Madonna while trying to free his cart from the mud.

THE ENCHANTED VALLEYS

Their allure has always inspired man's imagination. Rounded slopes set against jagged cliffs easily conjure up the rose garden of the mythical King Laurino.

THE LONG AVISIO VALLEY IS DIVIDED INTO THE VAL DI FIEMME TO THE SOUTH WEST AND THE VAL DI FASSA TO THE NORTH EAST: TWO NAMES TO DISTINGUISH THEIR DIFFERENT HISTORIES.

Perhaps it is the geology of the Fassa and Fiemme valleys that has made them the subjects of local legend.

The many types of rock indeed lend themselves to much interpretation and the different histories of these peaks and valleys are expressed in the various forms and colours of their rocks.

At the beginning of our journey, we spoke of how much the rocks tell of the history of this region: the Val di Fassa and Val di Fiemme are grand, open-air geological museums, a historical patchwork waiting to be discovered.

• Looking towards the Catinaccio

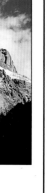

VAL DI FASSA
Canazei
Gries
Alba
Campitello
Pera
Pozza
Vigo
Moena

VAL DI FIEMME
Predazzo
Tesero
Panchia
Ziano
Cavalese
Castello

• Fortified house at Mazzin

• right: looking down the Val di Fassa from Sass Pordoi

the river, fed by the eternal glaciers of the Marmolada - and an abundance of wood, since the forest reaches also as far as the Val di Cembra and the banks of the river Adige; the wood industry is traditionally a large source of income for the people of the valleys. And then, the lofty peaks themselves: the Sassolungo, the Catinaccio, the Marmolada, the Monzoni range and the Latemar, the Sella massif - all renowned for their majestic beauty.

How can one sum up the valleys of Fassa and Fiemme in a few words? Broad and green, with the Torrente Avisio running through and the occasional village that reaches from the valley floor some way up the grassy slopes.

If you go up the road, you'll come to the woods of larch and pine groves from which spring forth the rock faces - in stark contrast to the lush greenery below - as they strike skywards, decisive, rugged, solemn yet somehow beckoning.

There is an abundance of green - thanks to the abundant water supply brought down by

SOARING SPIRES

of the Sassolungo (literally 'long stone') almost wittingly conceal the grand plateau of Alpe di Siusi beyond.

To its north is the Val Gardena, to the south the Val di Fassa. Feeling fit? You may like to try a guided walk along one of the sentieri attrezzati (equipped footpaths) or even the ferrate (equipped climbers' footpaths), which have iron cords and pins fixed securely into the rock.

● Equipped climbers' footpath

● Morning sun striking the Sassolungo massif

LIFE IN THE MOUNTAINS

centuries ago was very different from how it is today. Everything has changed, from the farming methods to provincial life. Yet the people are still very much united by their traditions. These age-old customs that used to unite whole communities have perhaps lost something of their original meaning, but the fact that they exist today is of great value in itself. While the precise history of the traditional dress may not be known, more importance lies in people having the opportunity to wear it, as their ancestors did over the centuries. In the same way that the rocks recall the history of a valley, a costume tells the story of a community.

T he Val di Fassa was one of the many areas under the power of the Bishops of Trento and Bolzano, which, in the 11th century, used Bressanone as their base. After the reign of the Hapsburgs and the Republic of Venice (14th-18th centuries), Napoleon ruled the area from 1797 to 1813. The valley passed under the control of Austria with the Congress of Vienna in 1815, but in 1866 it claimed independence under Italy, and divided into smaller areas governed by the local rules or 'Regole'. The Val di Fiemme followed a similar historical course, although here the remains of settlements date back to much earlier times. Similar to the "Regole" of the Val di Fassa, the Val di Fiemme was divided into four districts as early as in the 12th century, and the people constituted the "Magnificent Community of the Val di Fiemme", which was acknowledged also by the bishop of Trento. This independent spirit is a characteristic of the Fiemme people, something that gave substance to their resistance against the Tyrol and which succeeded in allowing them to retain self-rule until the arrival of the French, Bavarians and Hapsburgs, who overpowered them until the restitution to Italy.

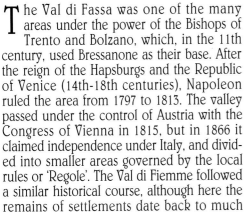

You can reach the Val di Fassa from one of its four adjacent valleys: the Val di Fiemme (SW), the Val di Ega (W), the Val Gardena (N), and Livinallongo (E) via the high Passo Pordoi, which, at 2,239 m, offers both excellent views and starting points for many footpaths or *ferrate*. A *via ferrata* (literally 'iron path') describes the footpaths with steep or even vertical sections that require a very good head for heights, fitness and some agility.

Local guides secure iron pins into the rock which are linked with steel safety cables. Climbers clip their snap-hooks and harnesses onto the cables in full safety. It's an system that allows thousands of day hikers and climbers every year to enjoy some of the Dolomites' most spectacular views.

Mount Sella, (literally "saddle") with its steep sides and table top is situated is a prime destination for hikers and trippers from all four areas. Known also as the "castle of the Dolomites", Sella's highest point is called Piz Boè (3,151 m). Two high-level 'valleys' cross the top: the Val di Mesdì and the Val Lasties (photo below).

Reaching the heights of Sella can be a tough enterprise if you want to go up one of the ferrate, but man's more modern additions have also made it a breeze! A cable car leaves from Passo Pordoi near Canazei up to the peak of the same name. It's very popular with tourists as, once at the top, they can choose from a wealth of footpaths.

Perhaps the most popular is up to Piz Boè but the lesser-beaten tracks are equally interesting.

A full-day trip is to cross the summit to Piz Boè for photos and a pack lunch and then walk down on the opposite side of the massif to the village of Colfosco. If you have more time and the weather forecast says "bello", you can stay up on the summit for a few days at the Boè refuge, and perhaps plan some half- or full-day walks and climbs around the summit.

Whether you're an expert climber, an excursion tourist or are simply craving clean air and a healthy sun tan, once up on the Sella, you'll be so spoiled for choice it'll be tough to muster up the will to come back down!

For those who prefer to take the cable car both ways, what better way to view one of the best panoramas of the Dolomites' most striking peaks than from the sundeck at the top of Passo Pordoi.

THE SASS PORDOI
The Sass Pordoi can be reached by a fast and modern cable-car that leaves from Passo Pordoi. During the summer it attracts both day trippers and mountaineers alike to take in the full panorama at the top. Situated at the very heart of the Dolomites, the Gruppo Sella sits apart from the surrounding massifs of the zone, like the throne of a giant towering above the four valleys below.

• A flock of sheep at the foot of Mount Sella

• left: the cable car makes its dizzy ascent to Sass Pordoi

• Sella, with the north face of Marmolada in the background

Notes

It's always a thrill to go up the Sass Pordoi by cable car: with today's technology, you are whisked up to the summit in no time: the double cable travels 8 metres a second, and the Pass is soon left far below. After skimming the golden vertical faces, you touch down in a unique world at the summit: a table-top landscape of pure Dolomitic rock awaits you, a terrace ablaze with unobstructed views of the most famous peaks. At nearly 3,000 metres, the air is fresh and giddy. Do the people down at the Pass know what they're missing?

At the southern foot of the Sella massif, at the northern end of the Val di Fassa is Canazei, a delightful village that can also be reached from the north (Passo Sella, Passo Pordoi) and the east (Passo di Fedaia). Canazei is an important year-round tourist resort because the adjacent mountains offer a full range of sporting attractions. Being only a short drive from Passo Fedaia (with its stunning lake) and the base of the Marmolada, Canazei is also used as a base for those who like to mix winter and summer sports, with the skiing on Marmolada being good all year round. After the period of political and religious dominiation from Bressanone, the Magnificent Community of the Val di Fassa grouped together seven municipalities (or Regole) under Canazei. Unfortunately two fires - one in 1854, the other in 1912 - destroyed many of the old buildings so that many of the town's houses and hotels are not original, despite keeping their Tyrolese style.

The district of Magoa survived the fires and is worth visiting for its typical architecture. Some of the houses date back to as early as the fifteenth century. If some of the Val di Fassa's cultural heritage has been lost, it is certainly made up for by the landscape.

Ascending on foot (in an hour and a half) or by cable car to Pecol's Belvedere, you can enjoy the collective beauty of the Gruppo Sella, Sassolungo (Langkofel, 3181 m) with its finger-like peaks, Catinaccio (Rosengarten) or King Laurino's garden and, of course, the Queen of the Dolomites herself, Marmolada (3343 m), with her eternal glaciers.

• Canazei and the Marmolada massif

WHETHER IN THE HEIGHT OF SUMMER
or in the middle of winter, Sass Pordoi (facing photo) retains its majesty and enigmatic aura. The cross on the summit is a reminder of the first alpine climbers to experience the thrill of seeing Canazei from above.

• left: the south face of the Sass Pordoi

• The old village centre of Canazei

CANAZEI
Is found at the northernmost point of Val di Fassa. At first glance, the road seems to be blocked by the mountains but instead to the east a good road snakes up to the foot of the Marmolada's grand glacier, while to the north a series of hairpin bends leads up the Pordoi and Sella passes to over 2,000 metres above sea level. The woods reaching down to the outskirts of the village are a testimony to the care the inhabitants of the valley take in preserving their nature. The villages seems to 'want' to occupy as little of the landscape as possible, leaving full reign to the grand old mountain.

The northernmost settlement of the Avisio river valley is Campitello, at the mouth of the Val di Duron. If the village's original raison d'être was to work with its water mills on the Duron stream, tourism has more recently superseded this activity. Nearby ski-lifts up to the rifugio of Col Rodella (2387 m) above Passo Sella.

Farther down the Val di Fassa is Pozza - with its fascinating mill called Mulino de Pezol - which today strings up the valley to merge with what was once the separate district of Pera.

Three valley mouths meet close to the village of Pozza: the Valle di S. Nicolò (E), the Valle del Vajolet (a couple of kilometres to the north) which leads up to the Catinaccio, and the Val d'Ega, leading up over the Passo Costalunga.

In the Ega valley, the mountains of the Catinaccio (N) and Latemar (S) act as splendid frames for Lago di Carezza, the unique lake with aquamarine waters and a shore-side village that leave a lasting impression on all who visit it.

Vigo is the largest village in the middle Fassa valley, and divides the resort area of Ciampedie (pron. Champedeeay) and the Costalunga pass, a paradise for climbers in the summer and skiers in the winter.

THERE WERE ONCE *many bears in the area, with the dense woodland and wildness providing excellent foraging and protection. Bear guards were even assigned, and it was a great honour to be given the responsibility of performing this job on behalf of the community.*

THE GRANDEUR *of the Marmolada, Queen of the Dolomites at 3,343 m (photo right), is overwhelming when compared to the world beneath her. From the top, the houses, cars and roads in the valleys look like miniature toys.*

• Botteghe (traditional shops) in centre of Canazei

• Old hay loft on the valley floor

• The spectacular equipped climbers' path to the top of the Marmolada

Vigo, the old main village of the Val di Fassa, is one of the seven Regole (the ancient land management co-operatives) of the Magnifica Communità. Some of the churches worth visiting are the 11th century sanctuary of S. Guiliana just above the village on the Doss Ciaslir knoll, which was reconstructed in late gothic style and has since hosted some delightful frescoes and three beautiful wooden alters carved by Giorgio Artz in the 14th century; the 16th century chapel of the Madonna delle Grazie close by; and the late 11th century chapel of S. Maurizio. At S. Giovanni, a district of Vigo, you can find the church of St. John, built in the 15th century on the site of a Roman cult, the remains of which are kept in the church apse. Also of note are the roof, which is very steep, and the slender clock tower, while inside you can see frescoes dating back to the 14th century. At S. Giovanni you can also find the Val di Fassa's Ladin Museum, or Majon di Fasegn, opened in 1981 in the converted parish barn. At the north end of the valley instead, from Canazei you can take the road for Lake Fedaja, which passes through the villages of Alba and Penìa below the Marmolada massif. Here it's worth visiting La Sia, the last water-driven sawmill of the Dolomites. Of course, during the tourist seasons the villages here are largely used as bases for trips up to the Marmolada massif.

AS RECENTLY AS IN THE LAST CENTURY *people sought out the adventure and challenge of testing their climbing ability on these peaks. The equipment used by like-minded people today is obviously very different. The distinguished gentlemen in the engraving (left) look dressed more for the city than the mountains, their composure reflecting the chamois goats, which venture up vertiginous heights with a similar nonchalance. Perhaps today's free climbers take their inspiration from both types of mountaineers.*

THE PUNTA PENIA (main photo) is the highest and snowiest peak of the Dolomites. With evidence of the last ice age still clearly evident, its glacier and permanent snowfields offer skiing all year round.
From the summit, the view is 360 degrees of unbroken horizon.

• Mountain goats grazing, and "gazing" at the glacier

left: the glacier of Punta Penia

• The Gran Vernel at sunset

This legendary massif (large photo right), standing 2,981 metres high, was probably given its Italian name by the farmers of the Val di Fassa, who called the large bowl below its eastern face *ciadinac*. In German it is called *Rosengarten,* 'rose garden', a name that probably harks back to the legend of King Laurino, king of the dwarfs, who had a rose-covered garden on this mountain. The story goes that no walled boundary encircled his kingdom; rather, a strand of silk, spun by the dwarfs to protect it from invasion. The good King Laurino decided to ask the hand of the princess Similda and sent three of his subjects to her court. But they were turned away by the Princess and mocked by the palace's guards - in particular Vitege, the perfidious chief sentry. On hearing the news of Similda's rejection, the King was so overcome with grief that he resorted using to his magical powers to return in person to the Princess Similda's court and abduct her. After seven years Similda's brother discovered where she was locked away and resolved to free her with the help of the stalwart Theodoric of Verona. They succeeded, but upon their arrival Similda told them she had always been treated well by King Laurino and that she wanted peace to reign between the two kingdoms. With everyone happy, only the evil Vitege harboured his malcontent, conspiring to make King Laurino prisoner. In the meantime, Laurino offered sumptuous hospitality to his guests and his dwarfs succeeded in foiling Vitege, who had plotted against the king and armed a band of his die-hard ruffians. But it was Theodoric's soldiers who finally betrayed the peace: a fierce battle was fought against the dwarfs which, with the help of Similda, ended in defeat for King Laurino. After a seven-year imprisonment, the King returned a broken man. On seeing the roses in his garden, he cursed them as the reason for his ruin. He forgot, though, that at sundown all the flowers would blossom, thus giving the Catinaccio that incredible rosy hue we see to this day.

● The Torri del Vajolet and the Santner refuge

IT'S A PITY

that the Italian name for this mountain has lost the legendary significance, although its modern name in Italian ("rough chain") is also very descriptive. In German it is known as Rosengarten ("rose garden") deriving from the legend of King Laurino, who tended his flower garden on this mountain. After the King was mortally wounded at the hands of foreign soldiers, he put a curse on the flowers that had betrayed him. He prayed that the roses would never again blossom at night or day, but he forgot the sunset. Today, during the twilight hours, it is said that roses come into bloom on the Catinaccio range.

● Near the Passo delle Zigolade   ● right: the towering east face of the Catinaccio

THE TORRI DEL VAJOLET

The hike from the valley floor up to the heart of the Catinaccio is undoubtedly one of the most popular in this part of the Dolomites. Once arriving at the top though, the sight of the tre sorelle ('three sisters') is enough to take your breath away. They have resisted erosion from ice and wind over thousands of years and still stand as powerful and defiant as ever.

The 'towers' are best approached from the west and the Vajolet valley (access from the Val di Fassa, near Pozza). The scenery is surreal, moon-like, and the walking equally enchanting. The views are of the Catinaccio (2981 m), the Torri (2813 m) themselves or, farther along the upper valley to see Catinaccio d'Antermoia (3004 m).

Notes

If you're thinking of doing any walking, you will need proper boots. Choose them carefully: for walking in the valleys, they should be low ankled and soft with a good grip; for walking on rock, you will need reinforced ankle sides and rigid soles. The choice of colour is up to you - what matters is that they are comfortable and suitable. Improper footwear is the main cause of falls and accidents.

THE BROWN BEAR
inhabited the area until the mid eighteen hundreds when the breed was hunted almost to extinction. Recent encouraging evidence of tracks has been found to the east near Sesto. Perhaps the bears have come from Slovenia and Austria, a glimmer of hope that the breed will once again roam the woods of the Dolomites.

At the cross-roads of the Val di Fassa, Val di Fiemme and Valle di San Pellegrino lies the charming village of Moena. Although it is officially part of the Fiemme area, the language spoken is of the Val di Fassa to the north. Known affectionately as the 'fairy of the Dolomites' for its own beauty, Moena is set in a verdant bowl with surrounding pastures, woods and peaks. The village districts are under the 'protection' of the Church of S. Vigilio, which watches over them from its hillside vantage point. A gothic style church, it was renovated several times but has recently been returned to its original structure, including the gothic apse. Beside it is the enchanting church of S. Volfango dating back to the 13th century and decorated with some very interesting frescoes.

The main road out of Moena leads up to Passo San Pellegrino, the vast ski area which leads to the villages of Falcade and Agordino. To the west is the Passo di Costalunga which you can reach either directly with a two-and-a-half hour hike, or by car by driving north a few kilometres to Vigo.

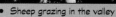

• Sheep grazing in the valley

• Towards Sassopiatto ('flat stone')

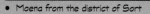
• Moena from the district of Sort

Predazzo and Cavalese share a common history as being part of Fiemme's Regola, or ancient property-ownership system. Predazzo, at the entrance to the Val Travignolo, has beautiful frescoed houses, some with gothic portals and windows. Cavalese instead marks the entrance to the Val di Fiemme, occupied a favourable position in medieval times for the clergy's domination and trading purposes. After 1800 the town underwent replanning and has since grown considerably. The 16th-century church of S. Vigilio and the building of the Magnifica Comunità are beautiful both inside and out. There is also a historic parish park where you can see the old parliament building, the "*banco de la rason*" where the Magnifica Comunità would meet on August 15th.

● View of the Moena bowl

MOENA AND CAVALESE

both mark the end of valleys, although they are situated on the river Avisio. Moena has an extraordinary location: behind it to the west, the impressive Latemar range; in front, the San Pellegrino Valley and the Cime dei Monzoni. Cavalese was only recently developed as a resort and it offers a full range of pleasure and sporting options with easy access to the Lagorai chain or Mount Latemar. During the winter there are enough ski runs for all levels and the village also hosts the famous cross-country ski race: the "Marcialonga".

● A spectacular view of the Pale di San Martino

● The ancient building of the Comunità

Notes

The building of the Magnifica Comunità in Cavalese is an important site of local heritage. It is still the seat of the ancient "Regole" which united the various valley communities.
The Comunità was constituted on 11 July 1110, granting independence from the Bishopric of Trento. The building as it stands today is more recent (14th century), with its frescoes by artists from the local school (photo left).

THE QUEEN AND CADORE

Nestling at the centre of its wide valley, embraced by rosy peaks, lies the unique town of Cortina.

THE SURROUNDING AREA - RIGHT INTO THE HEART OF CADORE - OFFERS GLIMPSES OF RARE BEAUTY, HISTORY AND CULTURE.

CORTINA
S.Vito
Cibiana
Borca
Pieve di Cadore
Calalzo
Domegge
Auronzo
Misurina
Lorenzago
Comelico
S.Stefano
Dosoledo
S.Pietro
Sappada

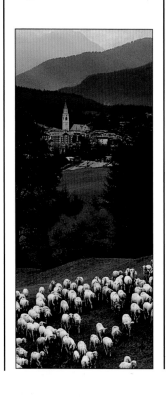

The Veneto part of the Dolomites reveals its secrets - at times of worldliness, at others, of reserved solitude. Descending the river Boite valley, you will notice much of the cosmopolitan spirit of Cortina dwindle as you come to Pieve, Sappada and Comelico, whose forests once supplied wood for the ships of the Serenissima Republic. Reaching this area - called Cadore - is now quick and easy due to the extension of the motorway from Venice and the widening of many of the main road's narrower spots.

Despite a long period of Austrian domination (1518-1805) Cortina and Cadore nurture very strong cultural ties with the Veneto region to the south. It's always surprising to note what a difference the 20 short kilometres between Cortina and Dobbiaco, San Stefano and Sesto can make in terms of customs, language and food. The Ladin spoken in the Ampezzo valley is also different from that of the other Ladin areas, perhaps because this district nurtured its independence as well as its contacts with more far-off villages as opposed to the adjacent zones. This is a feature which is borne out in the character of the Ampezzo valley people, who are

very different from the other inhabitants of the Dolomites. To this day Cortina retains its own legislative system, one that is unique in the Dolomites: the Regole d'Ampezzo. Based on the ancient Celtic structure of common ownership and management of property, the Regole stipulate that the 800 original families - or regoliere - administer the community's common land, which can be neither split into smaller parcels nor sold off to other families or outsiders.

The way the valley of Cortina presents itself today is undoubtedly much different from the scene beheld by the wayfarers in times past, when the forests reached much higher up the valley sides thus leaving a much greater surface for lower-valley grazing and cultivation.

The impression of coming to the Boite - or Ampezzo - Valley especially, from the much narrower Cadore valley to the south, must have been rather like leaving a narrow lane to walk out into a field. This was indeed how Cortina was recorded by the Dominican monk Felix Faber Schmidt on returning from a pilgrimage to the Holy Land in 1484. And his descriptions of the village as it was then are still valid today: "*Sole autem occasum petente venimus in pratinum, et est locus laetissimus inter montana, in* quo sunt prata multa et bestiarum pascua et in medio grandis villa..." - "While the sun was going down, we came to a meadow and there was a pretty place among the mountains with many grassy slopes and pastures. And, in the middle, there was a large village". Even if we have to live with today's traffic, Cortina has lost nothing of that same enchantment.

THE BOOK

above is a photographic diary that captures Cortina's unique scenes and moments. Available from good book-shops in the Dolomites, it contains a previously unpublished itinerary of walks, with both relaxation and exhilaration in mind. With superb photographs giving a close-up view of life here and the surrounding area, it provides a unique journey in time around a region that never fails to excite. Discover through the author's lens how the 'commonplace' doesn't exist, how life is the sum of infinite, unique moments. Come to know Cortina in her regal character, as she decides to unfold gradually, in her rarest aspects - but only for those who truly love her.

YOU CAN ONLY SEE

this view in September or October, when the whiteness of some early snow sprinkled on the upper heights contrasts with the fresh green of the late summer grass in the valley. With the town itself seeming to lie amongst the greenery, Cortina's clock tower strikes upward towards the Tofane massif.

• Inside a typical home

• The Becco di Mezzodì

• Cortina and the Tofana massif in autumn

• right: Cortina, Sorapis (foreground) and Antelao (right distance)

• The old Town Hall

Cortina is today renowned for being one of the Alps' most fashionable resorts, but its cosmopolitan atmosphere dates back to the 16th century during the period of Austrian domination, when the Hapsburg nobility began to frequent the valley they had acquired in 1518. This new influence gave the town an aristocratic flavour that was reinforced in the 19th century when it was discovered by English tourists who chose it as the most in-vogue spot for social and sporting holidays. Some of them became so enamoured of the town that they built their own homes here, like the Ladies Potts and Bury, who had a romantic villa constructed in neo-gothic style which was used for fashionable parties and the base for hunting outings. This background set the stage for Cortina to play host to the extravagance that heralded the onset of the era of tourism after the Second World War.

• Looking up the Boite valley with Cortina overlooked by Pomagagnon

AS THE EVENING

approaches, 'Corso Italia' is transformed into a multicoloured parade where families, hikers and daytrippers mingle with the rich and famous.
Many don elegant traditional costumes while strolling among the cafés, pastry shops, sports stores, antique- and art galleries, book-shops and wine bars.

YOU'LL FEEL ON TOP

of the world from the sun terrace of the staggering Freccia nel Cielo ('arrow in the sky') cable car (facing page).
From a height of over 3,200 metres, the houses below are reduced to white dots strewn among the grass and woods.

• Left: Tofana di Mezzo and the view from the platform at 3,224 m   • A concert in the piazza

Cortina is certainly not a resort for chic shopping and night life alone.

For many, the most attractive features of are found in the nature, preserved pristine between the sky and earth.

Mountain lovers will thrill to the variety of strolls, walks and challenging climbs.

The Cinque Torri ('five towers'), for example, is a climber's paradise with many different grades of climb.

They are reached from Passo Falzarego by chair-lift up to the Scoiattoli refuge.

The *rifugio* is also a great starting point for a walk up to the saddle of Rifugio Averau (half an hour), with its views of the Marmolada. From there it's another hour to the top of Nuvolau and the fairy-tale refuge of the same name dominating Passo Giau, the Tofane massif and the ledge-like Lastre di Formin. For the well equipped, there's the thrill of the "vie attrezzate" or "via ferrate" which take you to the unique panoramas that others can only see a segment of in photos.

One of the most famous ferrate is the "Punta Anna": starting from the Pomedes refuge (with chair-lift service), the path coasts along the lower cliff of the Tofana di Mezzo with some rather exposed sections to tackle. In the last stretch up to the breath-taking summit, the ascent runs parallel to the cable car.

• Equipped climbers' path on Cristallo

• The Mount Faloria cable car

THE SUMMIT

is a conquest. It doesn't matter that others have been there before: the satisfaction is indescribable. After hours of searching the ground in front of you for secure footholds, suddenly you reach the summit and are rewarded with a 360 degree panorama that reaches the farthest horizons - a sight to fill the heart as well as the eyes.

THERE ARE MANY

free-climbing routes and equipped climbing footpaths in Cortina. Trips are organised with expert local guides or, for expert climbers, the district withholds the toughest challenges and the biggest rewards: just you and the rock face, testing your endurance all the way to the summit

• left: the spectacular bridge at the start of the "Ivano Dibona" ferrata

• The Tofana di Rozes

Notes

Many have called the Dibona ferrata the most scenic of all the Dolomites. Take the cable-car up to Rifugio Lorenzi on Mount Cristallo.

The start is across an awe-inspiring suspension bridge (photo opposite), after which the footpath follows the crest with Cortina on one side and the Tre Cime di Lavaredo, Croda Rossa and the snowy Grossglockner on the other. There are also some constructions from the First World War. The walk takes a good 7 hours - tiring perhaps, but truly unforgettable.

You can drive up to the Tre Cime di Lavaredo along the very steep toll road from Lake Misurina. The first man to conquer the summit of the Cima Grande was the Viennese Paul Grohmann in 1863 while Innerkofler reached the Cima Piccola in 1881. The intrepid Dimai and Comici brothers then scaled the north face of the Cima Grande, a vertical and in parts overhanging wall which, until then, had been considered impossible to climb.

In 1911 Paul Preuss - who, like the Comici brothers, was a pioneer of free climbing - conquered the insidiously slender Cima Piccolissima.

The tradition of Alpine adventure began in those times and continues unfettered today. Today's equipment and techniques are obviously more sophisticated but although the pioneering days are gone, nothing is lost of the thrill of approaching these mythical peaks.

For walkers instead the best view of the three stone giants is from the Forcella Lavaredo (an hour and a half's walk from the Rif. Auronzo car park).

THE TRE CIME
di Lavaredo, seen above from the south with the famous Spigolo Giallo (yellow spur) of the Cima Piccola, are the Dolomites' most renowned peaks. Apart from their prestige in terms of sheer difficulty, the three peaks stand alone and aloof upon their scree-slope pedestal.

• From the Forcella Lavaredo

• Tackling the north face

• Mount Paterno, Rifugio Locatelli and the Tre Cime

• opposite: the Tre Cime di Lavaredo

TITIAN

(Tiziano Vecellio), one of the most important artistic figures of the 16th century, was born in Pieve di Cadore in 1490. He trained mainly in Venice, where he produced most of the works that today can be observed in famous museums around the world. Although not many of his paintings have remained in the Dolomites, Titian's legacy to his land was a profound influence on the style of many local artists.

• The birthplace of Titian in Pieve di Cadore

• In the woods of Vizza

F rom Cortina as you descend into the Ampezzo valley you can't miss the pyramidal Antelao (small photo right) towering above as you come to San Vito, a pretty village resort that has successfully blended its traditions with a stylishly modern square.

If Antelao is the highest peak in the valley (3,263 m), it is admirably complemented by Mount Pelmo (3,168 m) opposite: with its saddle-like summit, Pelmo is also known as 'God's Throne'. Many fossils have been found on its flanks, along with the footprints of the dinosaurs that roamed here hundreds of thousands of years ago (photo p. 106).

In quick succession are the resorts of Borca, Vodo, Valle and Tai, followed by the village

of Pieve. This is the heart Cadore and the birthplace in 1490 of Tiziano Vecellio (Titian), a true master of Renaissance painting.

The house he was born in is now a tiny museum for savouring those times and appreciating something of the art-ist's genius. An original painting is in the parish church.

• right: Antelao from the Val Boite

Costumi del Cadore - Ricordo escursione T.C.I e C.A.I.

The villages of San Vito and Borca in the lower Boite valley are sometimes overshadowed by nearby Cortina. Nonetheless, they offer the visitor excellent facilities and a wonderful setting: to the east, the magnificent Antelao, to the west Mount Pelmo.

lower Val Boite is worth a visit to see the paintings on the walls of the houses, some by renowned artists.

THE KING

of the Dolomites is a title Antelao (3,263 metres) rightly deserves. It is often seen with its "hat" on, a plume of cloud that the locals interpret as meaning the weather is going to change.

The villages have their districts close to the river banks, San Vito with its small lake and elegantly furnished centre. Mount Pelmo (photo below), with its characteristically horizontal rock striations, is a symmetrical block that surges up 1900 metres above the Boite valley to the east and the Val Fiorentina and Val di Zoldo to the west. The hamlet of Cibiana on the opposite side of the

● Antelao at dawn

● The Tre Cime from Auronzo

WITH ITS BELL TOWER

(right) was built in 1863, San Rocco at Serdes in the mid Boite valley was founded in 1626. A weather vane representing the Angel of Judgement stands atop, suspended in the air against the backdrop of the mighty Mount Pelmo. Inside the church you can see a grand painting by Jacob Bassano dating back to 1650.

In more recent decades, tourism in the Val Boite has developed quickly while San Vito and Borca have grown in moderation, without upsetting the balance between the housed areas and the surrounding countryside.

● Mount Pelmo from Serdes near San Vito

To the east of Pieve with the lake of the same name, are the villages of Domeggio and Lorenzago, with their pretty houses built in the characteristic style of Cadore. The larger resorts of this area are Auronzo, San Stefano and Sappada, where the vast green meadows and forests are enjoyed by walkers and gatherers of wild mushrooms, an activity regulated by the council to keep the edible ones from becoming extinct.

The village of Sappada is the cultural centre of Plodn, an enclave of language, customs and dress that are much more Austrian than Italian due to immigration into the zone of people from Drava in around the year 1100. With a distinctively northern influence, the cooking is also different from that practised in the rest of Cadore.

In the eastern Dolomites, to the north of San Stefano is the Val Padola and the district of Comelico Superiore. The villages of Candide, Dosoledo and Padola are renowned for furniture restoration and the slower pace of the tourist season.

The poet Carducci frequented these parts, which are much cherished by those seeking peace and quiet.

• The Marmarole massif

• Rocchetta Alta di Bosconero

THE WOODS

of San Vito, Borca, Cibiana, Valle, Tai, Pieve, Auronzo and the whole of Comelico share a rather more illustrious past than those of the nearby villages.

All the wood needed for building the fleet for the Venetian Republic was provided from this region. The logs were floated down to the Veneto plain on the spates of the River Piave, which were once much fuller.

Thousands of trees were felled and cut, to be carried down to the lagoon and play their part in the Serenissima Republic's era of dominance.

• Old haylofts, Dosoledo

On arriving at Lake Misurina it's as if the clock were turning back to the early years of the century. The atmosphere of the place, the landscape, the reflections of the mountains on the lake, the yellow-shaded hotel marking its southern end all seem to belong to other times.

We are taken by a nostalgia that lakes so often evoke, and we can picture the horse-drawn carriages or sleighs that once came up even in winter from Cortina, Auronzo and Carbonin.

The mountains surrounding it are essentially those overlooking the Boite Valley and Cortina, though of course they reveal different facets of themselves: the Sorapis massif and Cristallo stand aloof above the lake (photos below).

The lake - together with the much smaller Lake Antorno a short way up the steep road to the Tre Cime - gives a blurred, surreal reflection of the mountains beyond as the fresh breeze at over 1700 m playfully alters the images.

Rays of sunshine

glisten on the frost-coated moss; they caress the lake's surface and ripple through the reflection of the clouds (photo below).
On the peak of Sorapis the night's snowfall has been kindled into a million bright crystals.
The lakes of Antorno and Misurina are precious gems of the Dolomites, where the buildings conserve an almost melancholy hint of the early years of the century. The eternal beauty of the mountains is mirrored in the water; a vision of perfection and a place for inspiration, where nature's charm reigns undisturbed and man is enveloped in its magic.

• Cristallo struck by the early morning rays

• Lago di Antorno with the Sorapis massif in the distance

• right: the Cadini massif, its razor sharp peaks among the clou[d

THE PEARL

of the Dolomites, as Lake Misurina is known, hosted the speed-skating competition during the Winter Olympics held at Cortina in 1956. It boasts quite a wide expanse for the high altitude (1706 metres), but how else could it have reflected the grandeur of Sorapis?

LADIN AT HEART

So well protected between the mountains, the Val Badia has been able to preserve its lifestyle more than any other valley.
Contact with the Romans, barbarians from all sides, Austrians and Italians has merely strengthened this small yet large heart.

WITH ITS TYPICALLY TYROLESE VILLAGES, GREEN SLOPES DOTTED WITH FARMS AND TOWERING SPIRES WITH ROSY EVENING HUE - WELCOME TO THE VAL BADIA!

You can reach the Val Badia from four approaches: the Valparola and Passo Falzarego to the east, from the Val Cordevole over Passo Campolungo, from the Val Gardena over the pass of the same name and from the Val Pusteria to the north. This Ladin heart conceals scenery, legends, traditions and customs that go back thousands of years.
The valley offers a full range of tourist facilities, with pensioni for all budgets. The side valleys of La Valle, Longiarù and Tamores are hunted out by those who prefer a non-resort atmosphere.
Here you can savour an environment that has changed very little in the past hundred years.
From a geological standpoint, the valley's River Gadera marks the divide between the eastern and western Dolomites, which display very different characteristics.

VAL BADIA
Corvara
Colfosco
La Villa
S.Cassiano
Pedraces
S.Vigilio di Marebbe
La Valle, Longiarù, Tamores

The Val Badia is surrounded by the Sella massif, mounts Puèz and Sassongher, the Conturines chain, Sasso della Croce and the extensive Pralongià plateau.
Aesthetically it offers splendid views and sights of rare beauty for walkers and climbers alike. There are also two Nature Parks: the Fanes-Sennes-Braies bordering with the Ampezzo Dolomites, and the Puèz-Odle Park with the Gardenaccia overlooking the heart of the valley.

THE MOUNTAINS AND *meadows instil tranquillity and awe at the same time; the malghe (farm huts), houses and churches create an atmosphere rich in tradition.*

• right: il Sasso della Croce

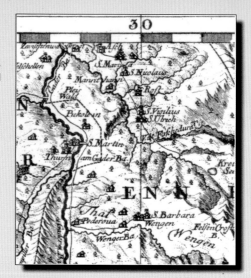

96% OF THE

Population of the Val Badia is pure Ladin. The folk take pride in defending their traditions, which seem immune from any influence from today's tourism.

THE MOUNTAINS

overlooking the Val Badia are magnificent especially when the evening sun catches the imposing and remote faces of these "pale mountains" to paints them with a rosy hue that deepens to a shade of violet. Surprises are always in store when you see them from a new angle or perhaps as the sun moves around, retracing their contours and reflecting the countless outlines in a captivating play of shadows. At the foot of Monte Cavallo still stands the tiny sanctuary of Santa Croce, dating back to the 16th century. With its incredible view and total isolation, it's hard to believe a hermit lived here in around 1000 AD!

Notes

Trained eyes can recognise which valley the people are from by looking first at their hats and then the rest of the costume. The real hats and clothes are not usually on sale to the public as they're handed down across generations. The villagers are true to their traditions and, in respect of the way things have always been, few alterations to the dress are permitted - only two flowers and a sprig of pine.

To better understand the present makeup of the people of this area - who are 96% Ladin - let us first take a trip back in time to seek out their roots. The dominion of the Roman Empire brought about the mixing of the local language with Latin to the extent that a new language was created and officially recognised as the Valley's third official language: Ladin. Many of the signposts here are in German, Italian and Ladin, since the proud people succeeded in obtaining official recognition of Ladin from the State, along with permission to put it on the school curriculum.

A dominant feature of this valley is precisely this defence of the local traditions, which, in an almost natural way, has made it an island of pure Ladin culture. Despite the history of the valley not being very different from that of the Tyrol, with the rule of the Bishopric of Bressanone first and of the Hapsburgs and Austrians later, until 1919, when the Val Badia was

● Sunset on the Conturines massif

passed over to Italy, the popular heritage has been preserved like a precious treasure chest, the lid of which seems to have only recently been pried off.

The local economy has also followed region's traditions: in the 16th century the people worked iron from the bordering valleys to produce arms for Venice and Europe; and in the 18th century wood was felled here for the production of ships for the Serenissima Republic.

And yet it seems that the Val Badia has been in some way impermeable to these contacts and has forged a very strong individuality. Another testimony to this is the Viles system, which are self-sufficient groups of houses that even today preserve a common fountain and oven.

fig. 76

● The standard bearer

● right: traditions upheld at San Martino

THE "VILES"

(pron. "veelays") are small clusters of ancient farmhouses that formed self-sufficient co-operatives. Corresponding to the organisation of the "Masi Chiuso del Tirolo", they are fascinating for their typical Badia building style and of course the materials used to build them: local rock from the surrounding mountains.

Notes

In spring and autumn, the people of the region come to San Leonardo to take part in the procession up to the small Sanctuary of S. Croce. There is a congregation in local costume, the priest, the baldachin (canopy over religious sculpture), altar boys, the band, and the sculptures carried on shoulders.
After a packed lunch everyone turns towards home at dusk. A day for the local people and their faith.

• The church and hostel of S. Croce in the Val Badia

The villages of the Val Badia today enjoy an intense tourist activity, due to a match of fabulous scenery with excellent facilities.

Until the 1930s very few tourists came here and in winter the pace of time slowed to wait the onset of spring and the return to outdoor farming activities. Today Corvara, Colfosco, Badia, La Villa, San Cassiano, Pedraces and San Vigilio have become some of the most popular of the Dolomites' resorts.

Yet perhaps the true jewels of the Val Badia are to be sought in the small and lesser-known side valleys of Longiarù (Campilltal), Spessa (Wengental), Marebbe and others, where the pace of life is unhurried even during the high seasons and where one can still hear the echoes of the past among people who hold true to the spirit of those times.

TIME STANDS STILL

Today, as in the time of the Hapsburgs, the costumes are true uniforms of the various villages. The rural architecture of the houses has also remained true to the old

styles, whether it be for ordinary or noble folk. It's not rare to see tiny villages of picturesque old houses with painted windows, nor is it uncommon to see groups of people dressed in their local Badia costumes as they stroll along the quiet lanes between one group of houses to the other.

Notes

For those fond of driving, within easy reach is a bounty of amazing attractions covering an area of over 180 square km. The Tabacco Editore map is an essential companion offering two possibilities of what to consult. On one side is the stradale or road map for choosing the best routes to approach and get around the Dolomites. On the other is a large panoramica map, ideal for detailed orientation, so you don't miss even the tiniest village.

● A procession in Pieve di Marebbe

A TYPICAL RURAL
house in the Val Badia, at about
1500 m above sea level, consists of
a stone ground floor, usually
planted solidly into

These timeless places are found in the Longiarù valley, midway up the Val Badia. Here are many old water mills on the stream from which the valley takes its name.

The mills are 'revived' for a week every August to celebrate the unique festival of the mills. Here, the 'viles' of a few identical houses clutch to the cleared valley sides, with footpaths and ditches connecting them, but many can also be seen at La Valle, where a very large and beautiful crucifix hangs on the outside wall.

The village of San Martino, close to the thermal baths of Antermoia, takes its name from the 11th century turreted castle that was reconstructed in the 16th and 17th centuries.

It's worth stopping at the small hamlets of the Alta Badia because of the fascination they evoke as 'true' mountain hamlets. Pedraces, the administrative seat of the Badia district council, is on the west bank of the Rio Gadera, with San Leonardo and its beautiful rococo church on the east bank. In the south west of the Val Badia is the Valparola, a broad, green valley that becomes a steep pass connecting to Passo Falzarego and Cortina.

San Cassiano has one of the most interesting rococo churches of the region. There are some charming old houses and a 18th century church with an interesting painted altar-piece by Karl Henrici. The valley also hosts the Ladin Museum.

Above San Cassiano is the wild Valle Armentarola, with a long ski run for medium ability skiers. Above is Mount Lagazuoi and the pretty Rifugio Scotoni.

La Villa, at the junction with the Val Badia, plays host every year to the Ski World Cup on the famous Gran Risa run starting from the top of Piz La Ila. From the top, other ski slopes connect up with the resorts of San Cassiano, Corvara, San Vigilio and Colfosco. Keen skiers can take even the whole day to do the "Sella Ronda" circuit.

the mountain
side, and an
overhanging wooden first
floor with a roof of slotted larch.
The cow shed - which was much
smaller on the higher pastures and
with the addition of a hayloft in the
'viles' - was a separate building to
the farm. The vila consisted of
about twenty buildings, comprised
of houses and cow sheds, and
usually housed ten productive
families. They were connected by
paths or irrigation ditches. Every
century the steep slopes would be
cleared of trees so that the pastures
could be kept for the livestock.
*   The most common cows of the*
Dolomites are the "Alpine
brown", the "Alpine grey" and
the "Simmenthal".

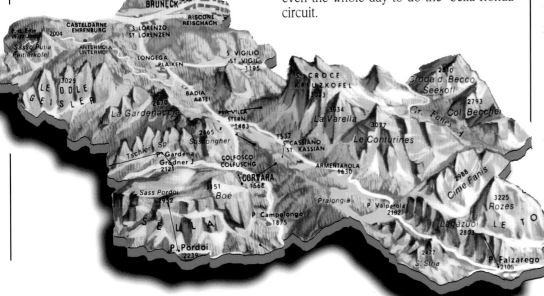

SAN VIGILIO DI MAREBBE

sits in a splendid natural basin not actually in the Val Badia but on its border.

The district is well known for its peacefulness and noted for the fantastic legends that Carlo Felice Wolff set in the nearby area of Fanes.

At the beginning of the Val Badia, at Longega, the road forks to carry on up the main valley or to strike east into the Valle di Marebbe, along the S. Vigilio stream.

Chair-lifts go up to the skiing area of Plan di Corones, which is also served by lifts from S. Lorenzo near Brunico and Valdaora. The Marebbe valley is gradual in its lower reaches, where the village of San Vigilio sits which takes its name from a bishop of Trento during the 14th century.

Administered by the nuns of the Castel Badia of S. Lorenzo di Sebato, today a religious icon still dominates the village, though no longer one representing political power: it's the gothic bell tower of the parish church, the current version of which being late Baroque (from the 18th century), although it seems that the earliest constructions on the site date back to 13th century.

The village is a blend of houses old and new, but it is adored by visitors for its enviable position between Plan de Corones and the Val Badia and its closeness to the totally unspoiled parks of Fanes and Sennes.

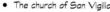

- The church of San Vigilio

THE UNUSUAL

asymmetrical cone of Col de la Sonè on the Gardenaccia plateau looks like a pile of sand that has trickled from the hands of a giant (photo opposite).

Nearby, the church of the hamlet of San Leonardo, dating back to the 8th century, stands out against the surrounding landscape.

Don't miss the interiors for the surprising wealth of their stuccoes and paintings.

- San Vigilio di Marebbe in spring

- right: on the Gardenaccia

THE BEST LEGENDS
set in the Dolomites, the Monti
Pallidi (the Pale Mountains) by
C.F. Wolff, would seem to depict
the Val di Fanes. Here, among
waterfalls, woods and desolate
peaks, the gnomes, elves, humans
and personified creatures such as
marmots and eagles found the ideal
environment for their adventures:
children being exchanged or abduct-
ed, trickery and loyalty, threads
woven to steal the light of the moon
and to brighten the face of the princess. There are promises and lies and
all the elements for making the
already enchanting Val di Fanes
even more fascinating.

BUT NATURE, TOO,
has its own magic to work.
Erosion has created almost the
same effects on the rocks as the
fairy tales: digging, smoothing and
curving the rock until it becomes
like a page of history, full of signs
and traces of an ancient past.

• Signs of glacial erosion

This mystical landscape, where marmots and chamois live among rare Alpine plants, is today protected as the Fanes-Sennes-Braies Natural Park. While wandering here, let your mind rove too, among the stone turrets, the rock forests and the wind-whipped waters of these Alpine lakes concealing the magical realm below.

Many legends have been passed down, sometimes partly forgotten to then flourish anew, embellished with imaginative adventures of new generations. Around the turn of the century, Carlo Felice Wolff devoted several years to the collection, reconstruction and publication of the local tales. Here is just one:

The last descendant of the King of Fanes was a lady who - to make sure the throne would be passed on - married a foreigner. While out on horseback one day, the newly crowned King found a young injured eagle. He was approached by the eagle's father, who was the King of men with one arm.

The eagle made an alliance whereby the King could keep his son on condition that he would be given the first born of the Lady Queen. However, unbeknownst to the King of Fanes, his Queen had secretly struck up another alliance with the Queen of Marmots, promising her one of her twins as well. When the Queen indeed did give birth to twins, Dolasilla - who was as bright as the sun - and Lujanta - who shone like the moon - the Queen was the first to make the exchange, and received in return a pure white marmot. Then it was the King's turn, who bundled up the infants so well that, in the pale moonlight, the eagle king mistakenly chose the marmot, which wriggled itself free from the eagle's grip in flight and escaped. The bad omen became manifest in a crashing storm over Nuvolao and Lagazuoi, where the exchange had taken place: so strong was it in fact that the squire who had taken the babies to the eagle took refuge in a cavern, unable to return. Only the mountains themselves know whether there is any truth in these stories; the rocks have seen everything and recount their past as they see fit, spinning the tales in the entrancing atmosphere of these places.

CASTLES, country houses, fortresses and aristocratic residences dot the landscape, their history riddled with invasions, war and power struggles that only the thickest walls could withstand.
Legends lie deep in the mountains' past, but there are also true stories of bloodshed dating back to more recent times. Being a zone of passage between north and south, east and west brought a price to pay for the area.

Notes

How can you see these places first hand?
Six km north of Cortina is the small car park at the foot of the Ra Stua track.
Follow the footpath first down and then up the valley about 35 minutes to the Fanes waterfalls (photo opposite).
For a full-day trip, you can continue up the valley, passing the small Fanes lake to reach the desolate area of the Passo di Limo (photo left) and the Fanes refuge.
While stopping for your picnic, be careful a gnome doesn't steal sandwiches from your hamper!

• left: the Fanes waterfalls not far from the Cortina-Dobbiaco road   • Lake Limo (2159 m)

CASTLE COLZ

at La Villa is very well preserved. Today a fascinating hotel and restaurant, over the years it has been the subject of many stories and legends, some of which bloody.

One which tells of a certain infamous inhabitant known as 'Gran Bracun'.

LIFE IN THE CASTLES

followed the rhythms of the seasons. The winter was spent indoors making utensils, musical instruments and embroidering while in spring the people went out to the pastures or down to the local village trade their wares.

be disappointed by the variety of hotels, pretty shops, typical restaurants and night spots. The older houses - especially at the southern part, which starts climbing the Campolungo pass - form the backdrop, all crowned by the Sassongher (photo left) and Pralongià. While the parish church is modern, the 15th century church of S. Caterina conserves gothic frescoes from the school of Leonardo of Bressanone and a highly prized wooden altar. For winter sports enthusiasts, the ski lift to Col Alt leads to a large high-level area that connects up with Piz la Villa and the Gran Risa run. From Corvara a footpath leads up to Colfosco along the pastures of Pentacosta and Costa. Colfosco is much quieter than its cousin down the hill, made up mainly of old, typical houses belonging to the Badia architecture.

AT THE BASE OF THE SASSONGHER
and flanked by the Puèz and Sella, is the village of Corvara. Delightfully tidy and busy, it has two districts of older and more recent houses. Here a full range of shops, hotels and ski-lifts cater to all budgets and sporting inclinations. Visit the parish church and the chapel of Santa Caterina with its late Gothic altar, which, with its depiction of the beheading of the saint, displays a trait common to art of this region of mixing the sacred and the secular.

To end our excursion to the Val Badia, our trip takes us to the valley's southern end and the popular resorts of Corvara and Colfosco, two villages which are separated by only a few kilo-metres along the road to Passo Gardena. Corvara is the main resort of the valley and as such adds its worldly spirit to the rugged views of the Puèz, Sassongher and Sella peaks. Here you will not

The 15th century onion-shaped bell tower is a delight.
In addition to the renowned skiing facilities for winter recreation, there's much do in summer with a huge choice of walks and climbs. From both villages, points of stirring beauty are never far away.

• Looking towards Sassongher

TOWARDS PASSO GARDENA
the road from Corvara leads to Colfosco, a delightful village that has lost nothing of its architectural tradition. Photo right: Colfosco chapel with its typical onion-shaped bell tower.

• Colfosco's charming chapel

• right: Sass Ciampel

THE LAND OF THE BEARS

The imposing walls of Civetta and Pelmo tower over the Val Cordevole and Val Fiorentina-Zoldo. Quiet valleys with steep forested sides and small villages.

RUNNING PARALLEL SOUTH EASTWARDS ALONG THE VENETO-TRENTINO BOUNDARY, THESE VALLEYS WITHHOLD MANY FASCINATING CONTRASTS.

The broader of the two valleys is the Val Cordevole, which begins just to the south of Passo Falzarego near the ancient Andraz Castle and runs down past Alleghe to reach Agordo on its sunny valley floor. The Val Fiorentina-Zoldo starts instead at Selva di Cadore to the east of the Val Cordevole, and reaches down to join the River Piave valley at Longarone, a town rebuilt after it was devastated in 1963 when a huge landslide caused the lake to wash over its dam and flood the whole valley.

The Val Cordevole and Fiorentina-Zoldo are known for their peace and quiet. A lesser-known area than others of the Dolomites, it has no large-scale tourist

*V*AL CORDEVOLE
Caprile
Alleghe
Falcade
Arabba
Agordo

*V*AL FIORENTINA-ZOLDO
Selva
Pescul
Pecol
Forno

resorts but nevertheless offers excellent walking and sightseeing options. Local handicrafts are very much alive here, and are based on wood carving and iron work, activities which have also left their mark on the place names such as Fusine (kiln), and Forno (furnace). The sounds of the artisans sawing, drilling, chiselling and hammering in their workshops do not frighten the woodland animals: in fact it's not rare to spot a deer or fox that has come down to the village boundaries. To see chamois, marmots and grouse, though, you should go up higher, perhaps to the small lake of Bosco Nero with the refuge of the same name. Wherever your wanderings take you, there is always a surprise in store, not least of which is to be found at Pelmetto (about an hour's walk from Forcella Staulanza) where you can see bands of fossils in the ancient sedimentary rock and the genuine footprints of prehistoric life (see p. 106).

The Marmolada is also the queen of the seasons, with the power to unite winter and summer under her sceptre.

The large glacier of Punta Rocca is open almost all year round for skiing. Accommodation is in the villages below or, in summer, in the high-level refuge. Holiday packages include ski hire, ski pass and lessons. In summer, the seasons seems to turned on their heads: make the most of the hot temperatures to jettison those bulky winter jackets and ski in your T-shirt. You will get an incredible tan but do be careful not to get burnt on the first day. The sun reflected on the snow is strong even in winter, so use good lip and skin protection. Once down in the valley again you can take up the usual summer activities of trips, hikes and climbs.

• Summer skiing

• The path on the large glacier

SUMMER AND WINTER

From June to October you can stay at the resorts of Lake Fedaia, Malga Ciapela or other spots near the foot of the Marmolada. Winter and summer sports await you under the allure of the eternal glacier.

• left: the southern face of the Marmolada

Notes

Whoever said you can only ski in the Dolomites in winter?
The Marmolada has a famous summer ski school, with lessons for competitive skiers between ski poles or timed descents starting early in the morning. From eleven o'clock its skiing for everyone (in T-shirts!). Spend the afternoon on the sundeck, playing tennis, at the swimming pool, working out or hiking, while the evenings are for barbecues and discos for those who still have energy left!

Like all places where legends are told, the Marmolada has become much more than simply a mountain. Behind every rock and crest and in the shadow of every peak resound the echoes of the stories recounted over the years.

Have the words been adapted to the stones and precipices, or has the topography instead been modelled by the pliable force of words themselves, as they have been pronounced countless times over the generations, like threads that bring us closer to the myth?

The Marmolada massif has a serious wartime history. The southern flank, like many other local peaks, was the theatre of bitter fighting between 1915 and 1918, and a whole village of soldiers' barracks was built under the glacier.

Today a museum commemorates these ordeals with fascinating period pictures.

This atmosphere - suspended between dreams and reality - is the one that climbers encounter as they approach the vertical south-facing walls. They can then marvel at

● below: the Bellunese face of the Marmolada

the Punta Penìa, conquered in 1864 by Paul Grohmann and two guides from Cortina. From the top, the silence somehow amplifies the power of the rock, the vastness of the panorama and the intensity of the sky. Seeing the Dolomites from this vantage point is a truly unforgettable experience.

The only companions for climbers or hikers in these places are the timid yet curious chamois goats that move in small herds amongst the upper slopes: with binoculars you can sight them on the grass or rock, sometimes betraying their presence when they cause pebbles to fall.

THE MARMOLADA,
the 'Queen of the Dolomites', is the highest massif of this region, reaching 3,342 metres at the Punta Penia which, together with the Punta Rocca - where the cable car arrives - makes up the chain that goes from east to west on the summit crest. The Punta Ombretta and the Sasso Vernale are also part of the Marmolada; although they are not well known by many tourists, experienced mountaineers are keen to test their skills there. The Avisio mountain stream or 'Torrente' dances down to the foot of the mountain to feed the delightful high lake of Fedaia (photo opposite).

HISTORICALLY

the village of Alleghe is one of the Dolomites' historical tourist resorts and today still lives up to its reputation. It is set at the foot of the imposing northern wall of Civetta and at the shores of Lago d'Alleghe. Although it's a bustling centre with many hotels, restaurants and shops, Alleghe has not been suffocated by tourism. In summer, the hay harvest still fills the air with the scents of an ancient tradition.

LAKE ALLEGHE

was formed in 1771 when a land-slide blocked the course of the Cordevole river, which divides the Dolomites into its eastern and western zones. Photo right: the northern face of Mount Civetta reflected on the lake's surface.

Farther north, beyond Mount Civetta, is Alleghe with the lake of the same name, mentioned as long ago as in the 12th century by the Belluno bishopric.

Some of the Val Cordevole's villages are built on rocky crests while others took root in more easily accessible points. There is much interesting local architecture, both in the hamlets and the larger settlements like Agordo, the most important resort of the zone, found at the feet of the Pale di San Lucano and Mount Agner.

To the north-west, along the road towards Passo Fedaja, is Falcade, a resort that successfully blends a traditional flavour with modern facilities. At the cross-roads for Falcade is Cencenighe (pron. Chenchenigay), originally known more for its iron and silver industry (once mined locally) than as a tourist centre.

• Looking up towards Mount Focobon

THE PALAZZO
Crotta-de' Manzoni in Agordo dates back to the 17th century. Venice's influence on the village can be seen clearly by the Serenissima lion engraved on the fountain in the town square (photo above).
The Baroque church boasts some paintings by Palma the Young and Padovanino.

• left: Alleghe and Mount Civetta

• In the centre of Agordo

CIVETTA IS OFTEN

is famous for its broad, 1200-metre rock face although the peak is part of a much broader massif that includes Moiazza and divides the Val Cordevole from the Val Zoldana. Hiking and climbing routes await sporting enthusiasts of all abilities.

Notes

How could we do without them?

The 1:25,000-scale maps by Tabacco Editore have always been the bible for hikers and climbers. Fully detailed, accurate and always up to date, they're an essential companion whether you're heading for an equipped mountain path or an easier hiking trail.

It's easy to gauge the differences in altitude and plan the best route to refuges, passes and peaks.

All the maps - which are numbered and divided according to zones - mark footpath numbers to make choosing itineraries easier.

Indispensable for finding your way around, never leave home without one!

The Val Fiorentina is connected to the Val Boite to the north by the tight bends of the beautiful and rugged Passo Giau, while to the south it joins with the Val di Zoldo and the Forcella Staulanza. The first village on this trip is Selva di Cadore, known at the turn of the century as Selva Bellunese. It's well worth stopping to visit the 15th century gothic church of San Lorenzo with its frescoes.

Forno basin. The woods give way to pasture lands, the valley sides become more gradual and sunnier, and also the views of the peaks change to take in the Tamer, the Pramper, the Talvena and the Schiara: new names, landscapes, contours and perspectives.
The hamlet of Forno, today a tourist resort, was originally a mining centre for the region, and to this day maintains its tradition of working with wrought iron, something at which the locals are true masters.

Not far away from Selva is Colle San Lucia. Both villages are part of the Civetta ski area and have grown considerably in recent years, offering more and better facilities for winter tourism.

Moving on southwards, we come to the Val Zoldana which occupies the Maè basin. Although initially narrow, the valley soon opens out into the magnificent

● The hamlet of Ornella

● The dinosaurs' footprints

● right: Mount Pelmo

SAN MARTINO

di Castrozza first became popular in the middle years of the 19th century, the era when many British mountaineers came to the Alps to claim the peaks. One of them, J. Whitewell, was the first to scale the famous Cimon della Pala (3185 m).

FROM THE SEGANTINI BAITA

Passo Rolle you can see both the Vezzana (3192 m) and the Cimon della Pala. A charming road leads up to the Baita amongst the pastures of the pass. In summer it's ideal hikers' country, while in the winter it comes into its own as a cross country ski area.

The origins of San Martino di Castrozza date back to the 11th century when it was a Benedictine hospice for pilgrims making their way up the Valle del Cismon. In the 14th century it grew quickly due to the mineral working activity while in the last decades of the 19th century it developed mainly as a popular tourist destination. Although largely demolished by the ravages of the First World War, the village was immediately rebuilt to become the fashionable resort we know today. Despite its growth, San Martino has succeeded in keeping its genuine character, local customs and values intact while matching them with the demands of its guests.

Its typical central 'piazza' sports a very picturesque church with bell-tower which is a 13th century Romanesque construction. Not far away up the main street are the boutiques and shops made of stone and wood, flanked by the larger tourism residences.

Perhaps the most striking features, though, are the natural ones. With the breathtaking rock faces of the Pale di San Martino. The peaks here are the Cimon della Pala - the most famous - and the Cimon della Vezzana - the highest - while the Cima del Focobon is found to the north east. To fully enjoy the area, you can walk along the foot-

path starting from Malga Fosse, which leads up to Rifugio Col Verde to then return down to the village.

There are many other panoramic viewpoints, of course. For example, once at Col Verde you can go up to Punta Rosetta; or, for the not-so-energetic visitors, from the opposite side of the basin, a chair lift will take you up to the Rifugio Toniola, where you can enjoy a cappuccino before walking up to the nearby Punta Ces. Then, by flanking the *malga* of the same name, you can return to the village on foot.

To the north of San Martino, Passo Rolle connects to the Val di Travagnolo.

The scenery is breathtaking on the pass itself. Both panoramas lie within the 15,000-hectare Paneveggio-Pale di San Martino Park, which contributes actively to the reforestation of red pines, which can reach 45 metres in height.

• The Segantini Baita

• right: the Cimon della Pala

THE MOUNTAINS

withhold infinite powers. They are evocative because, when close to their rock faces, we find ourselves thinking of eternity. They have natural powers because their resources have always been used by the people for sustenance or trading. They have mental powers because they forge our characters, making us resistant to life's difficulties. They have collective powers because they create a sense of belonging and cultural identity. And then they have magical powers: because it's impossible for rocks, pastures and forests to possess all these powers.

● left: the Cimon della Pala

Magical Mountains

We have now reached one of the most beautiful areas of the Dolomites, where the majestic mountains' reign is undisputed.

THE PEOPLE OF THIS CENTRAL LADIN ZONE ARE OPEN TO THE OUTSIDE WORLD BUT REMAIN TRUE TO THEIR 'GARDENESE' ROOTS.

Val Gardena
Selva
Santa Cristina
Ortisei
S.Giacomo
Pontives
Bulla
Castelrotto
Ponte Gardena
Siusi
Fiè
Laion

The whole area of the Dolomites is characterised by a variety of geological formation that makes it so remarkably varied in terms of landscape, colours, contours and vegetation. Yet in just 25 square kilometres the Val Gardena (Grödnertal) manages to concentrate all these variations: the pinkish peaks soaring up against the sky are flanked by crags of dark volcanic rock, or gentle tuff plateaux. The effect of this varied underlying geology is reflected on the surface, which, like the traditional costumes worn in the valley, displays a dazzling variety of colours and guises. The people, too, have a character that defies immediate definition: at times they display the reserve typical of the mountain areas while at others they can be very open towards outsiders, perhaps because many of the locals have also had to work outside area.

• Old barn in the Val Gardena

• right: the attractive resort of Selva with Mount Sella

• The centre of Selva

How could this valley be called anything but 'fortunate', encircled as it is by such impressive mountains as the Sassolungo, Cinque Dita ('five fingers'), Dantersass, Dente ('tooth'), Sassopiatto ('flat stone'), Alpe di Siusi, and, last but not least, Mount Sella? We can also describe the history and people of the Val Gardena as fortunate not in the sense that history has always smiled upon them, but that they have always been happy. Fortune indeed can be met by chance or actively sought and then nurtured once found.

The people of the Val Gardena are a naturally 'gifted' in this sense, having succeeded in 'exploiting' the beautiful scenery - at the beginning of the century it gained international status as a winter resort - while keeping it intact for future generations. Ortisei had already been a popular summer resort since 1860, while Selva developed as a winter sports centre, a role that reached its peak in 1960 when it was chosen as the venue for the world ski championships. With the construction of a scenic road to handle the increased traffic, the Val Gardena soon became one of the best equipped resorts of the Dolomites.

SELVA IS SITUATED
at the highest part of the valley at the feet of the Passo Sella and Passo Gardena, at the two sides of the grand massif. Today the village's most recent shops and houses are on the valley floor, while the older constructions are all perched on the sunnier, south-facing slopes of the Daunei.

Yet Tourism's discovery of the valley's jewels did not erode the Ladin spirit: the strong pride and individuality of the people from the Val Gardena have always gone hand in hand with an openness to the outside world, as if they wanted to display the natural beauty of the area while keeping its essence intact.

SHRINE AT SANTA MAGDALENA, VAL GARDENA
A Ladin mother, teaching her children to pray, stands quietly with her loaded basket repeating an Ave Maria, under this carefully tended shrine in the village of Santa Magdalena, in the Gardena Valley.

• Selva, looking towards Passo Gardena

• right: the Sassolungo

I t's no wonder, then, that the treasures of the past are jealously guarded and handed down with the popular traditions through the generations. Although the traditional costume of the Val Gardena is no longer used while working in the fields and is worn only for important occasions, it's also true that the right occasions often present themselves. No one would ever dream of not wearing their traditional dress to the festivals, dances or processions. It is generally acknowledged that the costume of the Val Gardena, called '*I guant da zacàn*', is the richest and most refined of all the Tyrol. Perhaps it's a reflection of the 'fortune' of its inhabitants, mentioned on the previous page. The embroidery, colours and ornamental accessories are certainly striking - both on wedding dresses and especially the maidens' costumes - even though they are no longer crafted at home as much as they once were.

The *Cesa di Ladins* (Church of the Ladins) in Ortisei is proof of the pride of the Gardenese people. The cultural centre of the valley, it hosts a folk museum with documents on the history of the local people, their valley and language.

M any people have left the valley to seek work in the towns and cities, but it is well known that a bond always remains, like a magnet pulling them inexorably back to their homeland.

CASTEL GARDENA
(facing page) is called Fischburg ('fish castle') in German, because Baron Engelhardt Dietrich von Wolkenstein farmed excellent trout in the surrounding ponds.
It is a unique example in the Dolomites of a fortified noble residence. Within its walls it has two masi (farm houses) with Renaissance arches, two houses, five towers and a chapel.

• The frescoed wall of a house

• Left: Wolkenstein Castle

Notes

Notes Oswald von Wolkenstein was a descendant of the noble family of the area who lived around the turn of the 15th century. He was well known as a poet, story teller and songwriter and reputedly had only one eye. A errant knight and man of arms, he had instigated the nobility to rebel against Duke Frederick IV of Austria. Legend has it that, while navigating the Red Sea, he saved himself by floating in a wooden cask.

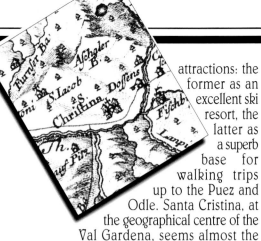

S elva lies at the lowest point of the Val Gardena, below mounts Puez and Odle on one side and Sella and Sassolungo on the other. It seems the district was already inhabited back in Neolithic times, while the village's existence comes to us from 13th-century documents belonging to the Wolkenstein family. Not far from Selva are the fascinating ruins of a castle (photo left) built by the Wolkensteins - the ancient lords of the valley - on two levels at 1600 metres above sea level, exploiting the natural caverns as rooms. Although close to each other, Selva and S. Cristina are renowned for two different attractions: the former as an excellent ski resort, the latter as a superb base for walking trips up to the Puez and Odle. Santa Cristina, at the geographical centre of the Val Gardena, seems almost the creation of natural elements rather than the result of man's work, such is the harmony of its position below Monte Pana.

Its older section is on the south facing side of the valley, while the more recent districts have spread in other directions in the midst of comely meadows, malghe, barns, and of course the chapel from which it takes its name in the middle of a meadow. The parish church is the main reason for the village's development, with documentation attesting to its existence already in the middle of the 13th century. With many - sometimes radical - changes being made to it in the ensuing 700 years, all that stands today of the original medieval construction is the bell tower with its late gothic spire.

Close to Rio Gardena stands the splendid Castel Gardena between S. Cristina and Selva, at the foot of Cianpinoi. Formerly Wolkenstein Castle, it dates back to 1622 and its latest renovation at the beginning of the century was the work of a Venetian baron.

THE RUINS OF CASTLE WOLKENSTEIN

are found not far from Selva at a height of 1600 m, on an outcrop of Mount Stevia. The castle had been built by the Maulrapp lords of Castelrotto earlier than 1225. In 1291 it became the hunting residence of the Villanders family, ancestors of the Wolkenstein family. The rock face acts as the inner wall and you can see the collection wells for rainwater and ancient horse stables on the ground floor.

• Santa Cristina in autumn

S. CRISTINA

is frequented mainly by enthusiasts in search of rugged hiking, but the resort offers the full range of attractions and facilities.

• The upper part of the Val Gardena (Grödnertal)   • right: dusk beginning to fall on the Sassolungo

THE ART OF WOOD-WORKING

is historically one of the Val Gardena's primary activities. Engraving and wooden sculpting began back in the 16th century and still occupy many of the valley's people.

The Val Gardena is renowned in the area as home *par excellence* of woodworking with a wealth of sculptors, engravers, frame makers, cabinet makers and carpenters. These traditional activities of the valley are still very much alive today. The earliest reference to an engraver in the Val Gardena dates back to 1580. Since then woodworking has continued and flourished, especially in the villages of Ortisei and Santa Cristina.

The techniques have obviously progressed with the times, developing not only in precision but also greater capacity to cater to the higher demand. The furniture, nativity-scene statues, toys, and the internal facings of the stube are sold in Italy and abroad. Many of the craftspeople can no longer be called 'artisans': rather, they have acquired the status of true artists who often exhibit their works of art at galleries and museums.

ALMOST LIKE A DIAMOND

in the early light, the Sassolungo emerges from the forest still shrouded in darkness. Later today many will start out from the base on walks and climbs. The view from those crests which seem to touch the sky is truly unique. The horizon extends well beyond the valley and the sun seems close enough to be within arm's reach.

The Val Gardena is dotted with many small villages that are worth stopping at if you have time. On the wooded slopes to the east of Col de Flam - the spur of rock dividing Ortisei into two levels - is the village of S. Giacomo, which is made up mainly of old farm houses or masi. Its chapel is perhaps what most attracts your attention: with its octagonal bell tower, it is perhaps the oldest of the valley. It is said to have been built in the thirteenth century by the local count who, during a pilgrimage to S. Giacomo di Compostela with his family, had a quarrel with a Spanish count. The reason for the contention was that his teenage son had fallen in love with the daughter of the Spanish count. But the maiden didn't return the feelings, whereupon the Spaniard had the son arrested, tried and even sentenced to hang. The boy succeeded in escaping the gallows with a ruse and, in gratitude to the Lord, his father erected the lovely church. A short way farther up is Stetteneck castle, which has become the subject of legends and stories of elves, nobles and witches. Perhaps the real treasure of S. Giacomo is the panorama that can be seen from its hillside church: Sassolungo (3181 m) embraces the scene, with its worthy courtiers of the Cinque Dita, the peaks of Punta Grohmann, Dantersass, the Sasso Levante and Sassopiatto (or 'flat stone'). Another village worth seeking out is Bulla, a typical agricultural hamlet a short way to the south-west of Ortisei.

Perched at 1500 m, it is found a short way before the valley narrows towards the Porta Ladina, the legendary house of Salvan di Pontives, the corridor that represents the access to the Val Gardena for those arriving from the Val d'Isarco to the east. With its gracious gothic church, Bulla emanates a spirit untouched by the pace of modern life.

AT THE BEGINNING OF SUMMER

(photo facing page) when the valley floor is already covered with luxuriant green, the highest summits are still capped by the last winter snows. It's a season to explore the heights, to feel the winter tide ebbing and the coming of summer.

OLD TRADITIONS

are a part of life here in the heart of this Ladin culture, whether expressed in the architecture, the signs on the walls or on the ornaments on the local costumes.
What's important is that everything is in its right place.
Here, the sense of order is not simply an aesthetic requirement, but a lifestyle where the homes, people and colours attempt to reproduce the natural perfection of these places and their landscapes.

• left: view from Mount Seceda   • The centre of Ortisei   • Characteristic leather belt

THE CENTRE OF ORTISEI

occupies the bowl between the Alpe di Siusi and the peaks of Rasciesa, in a precious balance between ancient tradition and modern life. The people hold on tenaciously to their traditions, which are expressed in the architecture, dress and the fascinating decorations of the façades, a reflection of the artistic sense of this valley's people.

Notes

**With its lace-like wooden gabled front like and Eighteenth-century dress, you can't miss the Hotel Posta Cavallino ('White Pony Post Hotel') in the main street of Ortisei at the crest of a rises that led to the village from two directions.
On one side is the central street for strollers, on the other the woods that encircle Ortisei.
An ancient stage-coach hotel, it's still just the right place to stop at for an espresso, a *cioccolata calda* (hot chocolate) or *aperitivo*. This is where you can feel the heart of the town beating, take time out to bask in the atmosphere and plan your trip for the next day.**

In spring, the village of Ortisei lies in an sea of lilacs among the woods of Rasciesa and the steep sides of the Alpe di Siusi, with Mount Saceda and Sassolungo in the distance.

Well groomed and pretty, its avenues have seen tourism develop greatly over recent years, without the influx detracting from its somehow exclusive and intimate atmosphere. The lower part of the town is a shopping centre, along and behind the main street. There are many colourfully decorated façades and botteghe (family-run shops) of woodworking artisans, sculptors and engravers.

The parish church dedicated to St. Ulrich - the German name for Ortisei - is on a slightly higher district at the foot of Mount Balest.

The village maintains a lively feel to it also in the low season because of its many handicraft activities. In winter and summer it becomes a hive of activity, with tourists from Italy and abroad.

Ortisei also has an ice skating rink as well as plenty of bars and cafès where you can sit for a drink while meeting friends.

• Ortisei from the upland hamlet of Bulla

• The Hotel Posta in the centre of Ortisei   • right: the peak of Sassolungo

In what was probably a place of worship in prehistoric times, Roman coins have been found up on the Alpe di Siusi plateau, together with remains dating back to the Bronze and Iron Ages. The Ladin and Dolomite legends state that a part of the Kingdom of Fanes here and it is indeed a magical area as it's a paradise for walkers and skiers. Lying at between 1800 and 2000 metres and covering an area of nearly 50 square km, the Alpe di Siusi is the highest and largest pasture in Europe. It has about 70 barns and farm houses distributed around it and offers excellent views of the Val Gardena with its peaks like the Sassopiatto and the Sassolungo (photo below).

In June this unique oasis of flora and fauna blossoms into a spectacle of colours, heralding the long summers days to come.
At its feet is the small village of Castelrotto (literally 'broken castle'), with its old streets and groups of houses around the

square and church. Although the village is much older, the name probably dates back to medieval times. It lays claim to a wealth of tales and legends, and the village festivals are renowned throughout the area: the procession of the via Crucis which leads up to the chapels of S. Vigilio and S. Anna is one big occasion for wearing the costumes, and the feast of Corpus Domini also attracts many visitors.

CASTELROTTO

owes its name to the ruins of a castle constructed in the Medieval

times and abandoned in 16th century. In the streets of the centre you can still admire splendid houses with frescoes and old wrought-iron gates, while breathing the air of this ancient place. Try to make time to visit the prehistoric settlement in the Laranza wood.

Notes

Cast your gaze down, leaving the grandiose dimensions of the Sassolungo and gentle slopes of the Siusi plateau, and stop when you see Presule (Prösels) Castle (photos above and on p. 14): small, with a pretty courtyard, high portico and frescoes, the castle holds suggestive concerts in its grand hall.

• Milk churns drying outside a malga

On February 14th everyone goes to the church of San Valentino, which presents an idyllic picture with its onion-shaped bell tower set in the midst of a snow covered field. Castelrotto was the administrative seat also of the western Val Gardena to which it is connected on foot from the Alpe di Siusi (from the Col di Palù for example), or by a short drive from Passo Pinei.

• Looking down to Castelrotto

• Il Sassopiatto and Sassolungo from the Alpe di Siusi

The splendid Mount Sciliar (2563 m) - to the south of Castelrotto and the village of Siusi - lies at the centre of the Nature Park of the same name. On a terraced part of its western slopes is the village of Fiè allo Sciliar, divided into its upper (*sopra*) and lower (*sotto*) districts. If you visit it, try to make time to explore its Romanesque church and the prehistoric settlement on the hill of San Pietro close by. The nobleman and poet Oswald von Wolkenstein used to sing his songs and recite poems along the road towards Castelrotto, and he is still honoured today with jousting tournaments and other country festivals. About one kilometre to the south of Fiè is Presule (Prösels) Castle (photo page 14); the oldest parts of the structure date back to the 13th century, but it was modified on various occasions. During the Renaissance period, towers and a surrounding wall were added. The chapel is late gothic and the internal frescoes are much more recent. It is very well preserved and is certainly a perfect complement to the romantic village of Fiè - the name also given to the lake at the foot of Mount Sciliar that is actually an artificial pond probably created by the Fiè-Colonna nobles to breed carp. In summer you can hike up to the lake for a chilly dip while in winter it's even used for ice skating.

• A late 19th century engraving of Mount Sciliar

RECENTLY

Fiè was finally given the name that suits its position: in 1988 it was officially renamed Fiè allo Sciliar (Fiè at Mount Sciliar).
Now the old masi and the pastures have their proper official status 'at' Mount Sciliar.

• The centre of Castelrotto

• right: Sciliar and the ruins of Osvaldo (Oswald) Castle

THE DOLOMITES ROAD

(photo p. 11)

THE ROAD

is mainly for getting from one place to the next. For the visitor, though, it can also represent an end in itself, an excuse for a car trip with a stop for a snack and a walk at the top of a pass. As the kilometres roll by, the road unravels its bundle of surprises, constantly changing the perspectives and views. While travelling, remember that you are following the routes of the original mountain paths and tracks trodden by prehistoric hunters (photo p. 11) and medieval valley dwellers.

Connects Bolzano in the west to Cortina in the east, passing the most breathtaking scenery of the Dolomites, amidst mountains, meadows, woods, villages - a unique blend of culture and nature.

ROADS ARE OF COURSE CONSTRUCTED FOR COMMUNICATION, THEIR SOLE PURPOSE BEING TO TAKE US FROM ONE PLACE TO ANOTHER.

But the Dolomites Road certainly isn't a typical road: bends, passes, many villages and constant changes in altitude all play their part in lengthening your journey. While for those in a rush these features are merely a hindrance, for the interested traveller they are the precise reason for taking this route: to experience a journey of changing scenery and discoveries. So if you want to cross the Alps in style, make sure the Dolomites Road is on your itinerary. Once on it, you'll soon realise how difficult communication between the valleys must have once been, with ascents of over 1,000 metres to the connecting passes. Originally these roads were only footpaths but gradually over the years they were improved to become the first cart tracks. In all weather, horses and mules were used to pull laden carts up the steep passes, to then tackle their downhill slopes, their hooves stumbling on the loose stones. Whole centuries passed before a cart track became a paved road, and it was only as recently as in the last century that an asphalt road connecting Bolzano with Cortina was finally constructed: over 100 kilometres of tight bends, steep ascents and descents - all surrounded by superb natural beauty. Always with something different to offer, it is an awe-inspiring landscape that unfolds before the eyes; an endless expanse of magical mountains, ancient castles, meadows and woods.

IN THE OLD DAYS,

travelling meant a tiring journey on foot, pony or being jolted for hours by horse-drawn carriage.

• The spectacular scenary of Pordoi pass

PASSO PORDOI

is one of four passes making up the high points of the Dolomites Road. It is part icularly renowned both for its height - a dizzying 2,239 metres - and panorama of Mount Sella, Marmolada, the Val di Fassa and the Belluno Dolomites.

14 Kehren tornanti

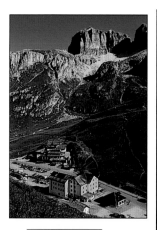

Notes

Why not take a walk from Passo Pordoi?
From the car park, go up to the small chapel and take the footpath up to the higher pastures.
It's an effort that will be greatly rewarded with the view of the Marmolada and its glacier, seemingly at arm's reach.
The best time of day to take photos here is late afternoon

Perhaps it's the thinner air or the older buildings up there which remind you of older times, and make you pause to think for a moment of all the people who have reached this point walking or on horseback. In the early years of the century, families and friends used to rent cars or taxis to come up for picnics.

ALONG THE ROUTE,

try leaving your itinerary to explore an interesting side valley. The view above is from Passo Sella looking down to the Val di Fassa, with the Marmolada in the distance. The summer offers a wide choice of walks, while the winter ski slopes have the right pista for all. And there are always the cosy rifugi, offering rest and mountain fare. The first villages in the Val Gardena (p. 112), are Selva and Santa Cristina and the Ortisei. Another option is to turn right, up Passo Gardena to Colfosco and then down into the Val Badia (p. 80). If you like driving, you can immerse yourself sweetly in the continually changing colours and kaleidoscopic perspectives of the landscape.

I f you decide to turn off the Dolomite Road for a while, you certainly won't be disappointed: between Canazei and the Passo Pordoi, you can turn left up to Passo Sella and enjoy the detour around the Sella massif, taking in Passo Gardena and Passo Campolungo on the way - a trip not recommended for sufferers of car sickness because of the seemingly endless repetition of hairpin turns and snaking bends to tackle. Passo Sella is a saddle at 2,240 metres that joins the Val di Fassa to the south with the Val Gardena to the north. It is framed by two of the Dolomites' most impressive landmarks: the towering vertical walls of Sella (east) and the Sassolungo (west).

The Sella pass also offers great winter skiing facilities and summer footpaths and climbs. The famous Sella Ronda is the name given to the ski circuit that encircles the foot of the Sella massif - a full day's skiing in winter!

In summer, the pass is a popular starting point for hiking excursions: one such example is the walk up to Col Rodella and the rifugio of the same name, a broad upland meadow land at 2,387 m. Once reaching the top of a pass, you will want to stop to admire the view and savour the atmosphere.

• Passo Sella

PASSO SELLA

links the Val di Fassa with the Val Gardena and separates the Sassolungo from the Sella. You can hike or ski, or go to the rifugio to try a local wurstel or sausage, or perhaps buy a few postcards.

• The road below the Sella Massif

• Passo Gardena

Moving on with our detour from the Dolomites Road, from Passo Sella we descend towards the Val Gardena. Two-thirds the way down and shortly before the village of Selva itself, we turn right to climb another pass: the Passo Gardena (photo above), which lies at a height of 2,121 metres between Mount Odle to the north and Sella to the south.

At the top of the pass, to our left is the Puèz-Odle Nature park, with the Odle itself (2,668 m) in the distance and the Piz da Cir close by.

From here the view of our destination is momentarily obstructed and we must snake down around a few bends to arrive at Colfosco before reaching the entrance of the Val Badia.

AT AN ALTITUDE
of 2,121 metres Passo Gardena - like all these Dolomite passes offers magnificent views. Spend hours of enjoyment here skiing in winter or walking in summer.
The ski runs are part of the Sella Ronda circuit, and therefore link up with the piste of the Sella pass. If you stop for a moment, you can easily imagine how quiet these roads must have once been, when horse-drawn carts were the only vehicles. Today, cars, motorbikes and coaches dominate the roads but luckily their speed is naturally restricted by the many bends.

• Looking towards Passo Gardena

*P*ASSO FALZAREGO
*opens onto the valley of Cortina.
On the left, Mount Lagazuoi -
unwitting scene of bitter fighting
during WWI - with its steep cable
car ascent to the top. Below
beckon the Tofana di Rozes, the
Cinque Torri and, in the valley,
Cortina.*

• Cortina with Mount Cristallo in the background

We rejoin the Dolomites Road by crossing Passo Campolongo to Arabba. Turning left, we head along the Livinallongo valley, with the north face of Mount Civetta in the distance to ascend Passo Falzarego, with glimpses of the ancient Andraz Castle down to the left. At the top, (2,105 m) is Mount Lagazuoi while to the right (photo above) is the Col Gallina and broad turret of Averau. While descending Passo Falzarego, you won't miss the Cinque Torri ("five towers") to the right and the stunning pink pyramid of the Tofana di Rozes to your left (cover photo). Shortly you come to Pocol with its enviable position on the Tofana ski runs above Cortina and, shortly below, after the small tunnel, to the full view of Cortina itself (photo left): on the left are Mounts Pomagagnon and Cristallo (3,154 m); opposite is Faloria and Sorapis; farther down the valley is Antelao (3,263 m), Mount Pelmo and the Becco di Mezzodì. Opposite, between Cristallo and Faloria, is Passo Tre Croci (1809 m), which leads to Lake Misurina and the end of the Dolomites Road.

• Passo Falzarego and Mount Lagazuoi

We have now come to the end of our tour and the end of the Dolomites Road. The landscapes - from the green meadows to the sheer rock faces - are fresh in our memory and our interest is still aroused by the unique names of the peaks, streams and villages. We have taken deep draughts of the light mountain air and every kilometre along the way has offered something special of its own. How many people have come along these roads? Up until recent decades, crossing the passes must have been an effort for the people and their animals. How many have toiled up them with livestock? How many left their beloved valleys, their carts laden with worldly possessions, to move perhaps only as far as next valley, or perhaps hundreds of miles away? How many have seen the views unfold

• below: the Lagazuoi cable-car station with the Tofana range to the left

which have then accompanied them every day for the rest of their lives? And how many soldiers have marched up these roads - even in this century - to reach their place of battle? The roads of the Dolomites have of course represented great challenges for sportsmen and women. Many cyclists come here to have fun or to perhaps dream of one day becoming a professional and competing in the famous 'Giro d'Italia'. This is where the race comes truly alive, where the teams push themselves to the limit to help their captain gain a prestigious victory. So, if you're in the area in mid June, be sure to ask

about the route the *Giro* will take. It's not to be missed: join in with the other spectators and cheer on every racer, irrespective of nationality. After the stage, the chalked writings remain on the road or the walls of the hairpin bends to preserve echoes of another epic battle - Vai Pantani! Forza Berzin! Vai Indurain! Whether we travel the Dolomites roads on foot, by car or bicycle, we must enjoy them: they have the power to fill one's heart with the past and present - and always with joy. Because the valleys talk about themselves and recount their stories and legends, from the commonplace to the fanciful. The panoramas unfold before your eyes like a film, and the names the mountains bear are so old as to be leading players of history. By passing along these routes ourselves, we like to think we have become a part of the Dolomites' history too, the latest arrivals in thousands of years of everyday life and arduous endeavours.

THESE ROADS

have much to tell of all those who have travelled along them. For cyclists they represent both the greatest challenge and the greatest reward. Despite - or perhaps because of - the steep roads, cycling is very popular, with routes to suit road cyclists and mountain bikers. But the Giro d'Italia (in June) is a multicoloured spectacle for all the family!

SPRING,

summer, autumn and winter - the roads are open all year round. The Dolomites Road leads us among the mountains and valleys. With its slow winding tracts mixed with and faster straight sections, it reflects life itself.

• Passo Fedaia

THE FROSTY VEIL

In winter a white veil descends on the mountains, creating an new, surreal world - familiar yet foreign. The towns and refuges glow, the wine is mulled, chilly thrills await you in the morning on the ski runs: welcome to winter in the Dolomites.

FROM THE LIVELIEST RESORTS TO THE MOST ISOLATED VALLEYS, THE SNOW - WINTER'S QUEEN IN THE DOLOMITES - NOW REIGNS SUPREME OVER MOUNTAINS, VALLEYS, HOUSES AND PEOPLE

AT SUNSET
the light's reflection on the snow creates extraordinary effects that enhance the rosy splendour of these mountains.
Then, as the light dwindles, the twilight air becomes so cold it seems that the snow emits ice itself. Luckily, the glowing light from houses, shop windows and street lamps reminds us of the warm rosy hues of the rocks at sundown.

While touring the Dolomites in summer, you'll of course feel as though you know the valleys and peaks you visited. Yet on returning - as you must - in winter, you may not even recognise the place you had stayed in! As if you were arriving for the first time, the snow changes everything and the places that were once familiar are now eerily altered. The people also change in winter, but not only because some tourists don't come here in summer. The summer months are marked by the infectious laughter of the refuges, picnics in the woods and conversation on the sunny banks

of streams which seem themselves to be joining in the merriment; in winter we become more reserved, almost as if our own silence was a reflection of the awe-inspiring white stillness enshrouding the land. Only the home-made sausages, soups and aromatic grappa of the refuges succeed in softening our mood especially when shared in good company and in front of a warm hearth. The mountains, too, seem to share this initially reticent disposition: everything is more still, softer, muffled as if the snow's weight had become infinitely heavy under the spell from the sky, and the rocks were destined never to be free again. But when we're out on the ski slopes, our cheerful spirit returns: the concentration of fitting our ski boots, the first turns, the colours, the laughs, the people, movement and company. A thousand zigzagging dots having fun - for some, even more than in summer!

Every year the Tofana's 'Olimpia' run plays host to the women's World Ski Cup. Highlight of the weekend is seeing the downhill specialists tackling the awesome Pomedes run by skiing straight down it! Another cable car takes you up to the high-level Ra Valles ski bowl, with access to the famous black run, the Forcella Rossa with its impossible moguls. All the main runs are supplied with artificial snow, and so are open from mid December to mid April.

SKIING

seems to be an activity that evolved naturally in Cortina, especially if you consider that the earliest runs were opened in the early years of this century. First there were large sledges towed by strong ropes, then the early cable cars. The Faloria station - which dates back to the Thirties but has recently been completely renovated - takes you from the centre of town to a district with runs catering to all levels. Its north-facing alignment means the snow is good right through until April.

Cortina is as much a paradise in winter as in summer: the same cosmopolitan milieu rush to enjoy the unique mix of urban and Alpine attractions found here - from the ski runs to the pastry cafès and chic night clubs. Some sports enthusiasts shun the night-life to go to bed early, ready to unleash their energy the following morning on the downhill slopes or on Alpine ski excursions. As previous host to the winter Olympics, Cortina is everything you expect from a winter resort. The ice rink for skating or watching a game of hockey; the bobsled run, with a taxi-bob service for those with strong nerves. Then there are the cross-country tracks at Fiammes, Misurina and along the Val di Landro, where the old railway line is now a trail connecting Cortina with Dobbiaco.

Most of all, there are the downhill ski slopes, on all sides of the bowl and for all levels and tastes: just the names of Tofana, Faloria, Cristallo, Lagazuoi, and Cinque Torri get the adrenaline flowing in anyone who's ever skied them. Not far away is San Vito and Borca, with their runs on the slopes of Mount Antelao.

● The Tondi ski slopes, Faloria

● The centre of Cortina in the evening

● Cortina and the Tofane massif

Overall the ski district of Cortina, Misurina, San Vito and Borca offers over 130 km of downhill ski runs while for cross country enthusiasts there are about 70 km.

The Lagazuoi cable car takes you to the top of a 10 km run all the way to Armentarola (but stop at the Scottoni refuge half way!) and the Val Badia. If you leave early, you can ski at La Villa and Corvara or, by taking the famous 'four passes' route, even Arabba. Make sure your day ski-pass is valid for the Dolomiti Superski area.

● Jumping in powder snow

● The Faloria cable-car

● The ski slopes leading from Pordoi to Arabba

● Sled-dog race

A rabba is another paradise for skiers, whether they be down-hillers, Alpine powder lovers or cross-country excursionists. In all the district offers 24 ski-lifts and about 50 kilometres of slopes.
For beginners, there are the family runs of Passo Pordoi and Pralongià (on Passo Campolungo above Corvara).
The more expert skiers head for the modern lifts of Porta Vescova above the village which take you up to the district of red- and black-category descents. The scenery is spectacular and the Marmolada can be both seen and approached.
Arabba is also on the route of the 'Sella Ronda', the circuit (or *giro*) of the four passes (Pordoi, Sella, Gardena and Campolungo) which embraces the Sella massif.

For those yearning for snow, silence, walking, and off-piste skiing, the area offers various Alpine ski excursions. With its cross country tracks in the valley, such an extensive ski district makes Arabba a varied and important winter resort.

THE SKI RUNS

of Arabba are connected to the 'Sella Ronda' and thus give access to other ski districts in the Val Badia, Val Gardena, Val di Fassa and Marmolada.
By taking the ski-bus, you can even arrive at Cortina.

Notes

A somewhat hair-raising experience awaits you at Cortina's Olympic taxi-bobsled. You can have a photo taken of your green-tinged grimace at one of those points when it's too late to turn back! Another great sport is snowshoe walking (with rental from Lino Lacedelli's 'K2' sport shop). At Misurina, polo tournaments are held on the snow field (where, rather than tea, mulled wine is much more in order).
For all your photographic needs, the best advice is from Foto Zardini in the square below the bell tower.

S an Martino di Castrozza, the Fassa and Fiemme valleys and the Moena-Falcade slopes make up the south-western ski district of the Dolomites.

From the Tognola slopes, you can see the Pale di San Martino just over the bowl. Then there are the slopes of the Passo Rolle, where there is also a ski jump.

The area of the Val di Fiemme has many slopes, especially around Predazzo. While Cavalese has a group of its own runs on Mount Cernis, from Predazzo you can cross Mount Latemar from east to west and arrive at the Obereggen circuit (both belong to the Superski pass).

Going north, the Val di Fiemme is well known for its cross-country skiing trails, which run along the valley floor through Pozza, Mazzin, Fontanazzo and Campitello to as far as Canazei. The Fassa and Fiemme valleys host the famous annual Marcialonga cross-country race, a hugely popular event which starts from Moena.

In the Val di Fassa, the villages of Vigo and Pera are the launching pads up to the Ciampedie slopes.

Then there are the passes of Costalunga, S. Pellegrino, Valles and the Alpe Lusia, which are partly connected and all covered again by the Dolomite Superski pass.

THE MARCIALONGA

(literally 'long march'), which is held in January and starts from Moena, is one of the most famous cross-country races, not least because it takes in 70 km of splendid countryside of the Fassa and Fiemme valleys. Although the home of cross-country skiing, there are many downhill skiing resorts, like Canazei, with its nearby slopes of Belvedere-Pordoi, Campitello-Col-Rodella-Sella, Alba and Marmolada.

THE SELLA RONDA

is a circuit of downhill slopes (medium to advanced, depending on your choice) that encircle the Sella massif. You can spend the whole day skiing without having to repeat the same run. With Mount Sella as your constant backdrop your trip will take in 360 degrees of spectacular Dolomite scenery.

● The Marcialonga

● From the top of Sass Pordoi

The Val Gardena's scenery in winter is like a Christmas card come alive: rustic architecture, horse-drawn sleighs, bustling movement lights and colours, dense woodland, white blanketed pastures, framing snowy peaks - and all with ski runs that come to within a few metres from the houses.

The Val Gardena is well used to catering to tourism, and in addition to the terrific mountain slopes, it also provides visitors with the full range of winter facilities. There are four main centres, which connect partly to each other: first, north of Ortisei and S. Cristina is the Rasciesa-Saceda-Col Raiser area with its medium-difficulty runs and awe-inspiring panoramas of Mounts Sassolungo, Sella, Catinaccio and Odle. Next, on the south side of the valley is the Alpe di Siusi plateau, with great panoramas for downhill enthusiasts (beginner to 'blue' slopes) as well as a full range of cross-country trails and strolls.

The third area is the district above Selva and Passo Gardena called Dantercepies, which has medium and difficult runs as well as many beginner slopes in its lower parts.

• The centre of Ortisei in the evening

• The slopes of Selva

ON THE SLOPES OR IN POWDER SNOW.

The Val Gardena has kilometres of slopes for downhill and cross-country skiing. All the downhill runs touch the Sella Ronda circuit so you can connect up to the adjacent valleys on the same day. The panoramas are extraordinary and the ski lifts are so close to the village centres that you can put your skis on at the hotel door!

THE SUN AT HIGH LEVELS

gives a deep tan in the mountains and, in the Val Gardena - an area known for attracting the real mountain enthusiasts - people don't mind taking time off to relax in the sun. One is never far from a warm 'rifugio', so the choice really depends on the view you want to enjoy as you drink a beer or enjoy a 'panino con salsiccia' (sausage roll)!

The fourth main area is the Ciampinoi-Plan and Monte Pana district above S. Cristina and Selva, which has many connected slopes for all levels, and a steep descent used by the World Ski Cup for the more expert skiers.
The villages also have ice-skating rinks and a total of over 100 km of cross-country trails for tourists and athletes alike.
The zone's popularity means you will sometimes have to queue up for the ski lifts but its well worth the wait!

• Wolkenstein Castle under fresh snow

ALONG THE WOODS

of the Valle di S. Cassiano, those who descend from Armentarola in the district of the same name can take the horse-drawn sleighs to reach S. Cassiano or be towed on skis by a rope tied to the sleigh for a few hundred metres. The slopes on the Pralongià plateau are all connected among them and also join up with the villages of Corvara, La Villa and San Cassiano.

You can ski to the Val Badia from the east down the 10-km slope from Lagazuoi to Armentarola and San Cassiano, and then to La Villa, where the cable car leads up to Piz la Villa; once at the top, you can either tackle the legendary Gran Risa slope - one of the most beautiful runs of the World Cup races - or cross the easy slopes on the plateau to Pralongià, above Passo Campolungo. If your legs up to it, you can embark on the day-long Sella Ronda circuit.

There are three main ski districts in the Val Badia: Passo Gardena/Colfosco - part of the Sella Ronda - with easy slopes; Pralongià, with its splendid panoramas and intricate web of slopes; and Sella-Boè, which is reached from Corvara and Passo Campolongo.

It has an expert run at the top and a range of blue and red slopes lower down.
On the valley floor are many circuits for cross-country skiers. The liveliest resort is Corvara, which offers a full range of shopping and entertainment - from Ladin specialities to international fashion.

MODERN SKI LIFTS

take waves of sporting enthusiasts up to the snow. In the Val Badia, the local traditions are not neglected and, valley snow permitting, even the locals take trips on sleighs at the foot of Pralongià to evoke times gone by.

• Near Colfosco

• The Piz la lla cable car

• Ski lift to the foot of Sasso della Croce at Pedraces, Val Badia

entrance to the Val di Sesto; from the main valley leads the Val Fiscalina, which has some easy ski slopes and offers excellent views of the Tre Cime di Lavaredo.

From Dobbiaco a cross-country trail following the tracks of the abandoned railway line lead all the way to Cortina. It runs below the precipices of Mounts Ludo and Landro and along the icy shores of Lago di Landro (Durrensee) with views of Cristallo, Croda Rossa, and the Tre Cime.

Although this is definitely the land of cross-country skiing, the downhill slopes of Plan de Corones, above Brunico, and Mount Elmo above San Candido and Sesto, are very popular - and rightly so: Plan de Corones vaunts over 90 km of slopes for various levels, which are steeper on the Brunico side

CROSS-COUNTRY
skiing reigns undisputed in the Val Pusteria. Over 200 km of trails run from the Val Fiscalina near Sesto all the way to Cortina and Valdaora, and all with splendid scenery and crisp mountain air

I f you are looking for some tranquillity, we highly recommend the Val Pusteria, a veritable winter retreat. Its woods, gentler slopes and Tyrolese villages offer ideal surroundings for cross-country skiers, with over 200 km of trails to choose from. S. Vigilio di Marebbe is a good base to start from on the paths that lead into the Sennes-Fanes Natural Park, a pristine zone offering forest trails and inviting rifugi. The Valdaora too offers trails which join up with the Val Pusteria, with its circuit which extends the entire length of the valley.

At the eastern end of the Val Pusteria is the

and easier towards Valdaora. Mount Elmo instead has over 40 km of downhill slopes with modern ski lifts.

Finally, the Alta Pusteria valley has much to offer for Alpine ski excursionists, but you can enjoy many other exciting activities here: horse trekking is popular, as are the spectator sports of ski jumping and husky races.

to fill your eyes as well as your lungs. For those who enjoy a long peaceful trek on foot or skis, you couldn't ask for a better place than the Val Pusteria. The side valleys are perfect for Alpine ski excursions, and local guides can lead you to some truly fascinating places, far removed from any remnant of civilisation.
For sports enthusiasts or spectators, there are the downhill and cross-country races, like the Cortina-Dobbiaco.

Notes

Why not go and see the colours and movement of a long cross-country ski race?
In addition to the world-renowned Marcialonga, the Pustertaler Marathon and the Cortina-Dobbiaco are two races you won't want to miss!
The Cortina-Dobbiaco follows the old railway line and has a spectacular finish in the centre of Cortina.
For tourists, the trails are open to the public, so you can ski them for yourselves to see if you've got what it takes to 'go pro'!

And if you want to have a go in the race proper, make sure you sign up well in advance to get a low start number.

• The long distance cross country "Dobbiaco-Cortina" race

GLOSSARY

The period photographs have been taken mainly from the private archive and historical collection of 'Foto Zardini', Cortina.

Other photographs, drawings, maps, relief maps, engravings, water-colours, chromolithography are from:

Tabacco Editore, Udine.
l'Encyclopedie, 1762
Deutsche verlags unstslt, 1899
Johan Schreiber, 1880
E. Harrison Compton
Peter Anic - Atlas Tyrolensis 1700
Breveglieri - Belluno
A.A.Paine-Tyrol und Voralberg
Johann Bergauner, 1850
Mataeus Merian
Meyers Konversations lexicon - Lipzig, 1897
L.M. Davidson-Seeley service - London 1828
Joch. Amonn- Bolzano 1922
Purger & C. München, 1899
"Amici del museo" - Selva di Cadore

Aerial photographs are authorised by the S.M.A.

The criteria adopted for dividing the chapters of this guide reflect the free interpretation of the authors and in no way correspond to political and administrative boundaries or geographical and linguistic zones.
The authors would most appreciate being notified of any inaccuracies, which will be corrected in future editions

- This page: the Punta Marietta (Tofana di Rozes)
- Cover photo: the Tofana di Rozes at dawn

alpeggio	mountain pasture
baita	mountain hut
bivacco	small metal hut
botteghe	family-run shops
cabinovia	gondola lift (enclosed)
camere	rooms to let (guest-house sign)
camoscio	chamois goat
capriolo	small roe deer
cardo	thistle
cervo	large deer
cima	summit or peak
croda	crag
destra	right
ferrata (via)	equipped climbing path
fiume	river
forcella	high pass, col or saddle
funivia	cable car
fuori-pista	off-piste or power skiing
gruppo	massif, group or chain
maestro di sci	ski instructor
malga	mountain dairy farmhouse
maniero	castle or country house
maso	valley farmhouse
Maso chiuso	Austro-Germanic system of primogeniture originating in the 16th century.
massiccio	massif
monte	mount
noleggio	hire, rental
osteria	inn
ovovia	gondola or bubble-car lift
Parco Naturale	literally "Natural Park"
pensione	guest house
pista	ski run or slope
piz	Ladin for summit or peak
rallentare	"slow down" (road sign)
Regole	The "Regole" co-operative land management system, originating in the 12th century, to limit subdivision or reassignment. There are 11 Regole and 800 families.
rifugio	refuge (a café, with accommodation depending on the season)
rio	stream, brook
riparazioni sci	ski repair
sasso	stone, rock or "mount"
sci di fondo	cross-country skiing
seggiovia	chair lift
sentiero	footpath, trail
sentiero attrezzato	footpath equipped with iron cords (see page 47)
sinistra	left
stambecco	long-horned wild mountain goat
stube	living room (German)
tornante	hairpin bend, switchback (road sign)
torrente	mountain stream
ultima discesa	last ride down
ultima salita	last ride up
val	valley
valanga	avalanche
via	road, route
via ferrata	literally "iron way", a steep footpath with iron cables to clip climbers' harnesses onto (see page 47).
vietato	prohibited, forbidden